FOR GOD ALONE

FOR GOD ALONE

Devotional Thoughts From The Writings Of

CATHERINE BOOTH

Compiled by

NORMAN ARMISTEAD

Ambassador

For God Alone
Copyright © 1990 Norman Armistead

Printed and published by
AMBASSADOR PRODUCTIONS LTD.
PROVIDENCE HOUSE
16 Hillview Avenue,
Belfast, BT5 6JR.

37 Leconfield Road,
Loughborough
Leics. LE11 3SP

ISBN 0 907927 56 4

Index

INDEX

INDEX

DEDICATION

To my mother,
another Catherine,
with love and gratitude.

In the preface of my biography of Catherine Booth, my grandmother and the first woman salvationist, known as the Mother of The Salvation Army, I expressed the hope that the book might be a telescope bringing her into focus for people today. As I prepared the book I lived in her thoughts, searched out her motives, and became familiar with her idiosyncrasies. My pulse quickened as I considered her zeals and I longed that the book might inspire and challenge the youth of today to commit themselves to the service of Christ in the certainty that *'God is enough for us'*.

I was only a child of seven when she was promoted to Glory in 1890. Now, almost 100 years on, I am sure she has much to say to a new generation; her influence lives on through her writings. My hope is renewed that some may be called of God to dedicate themselves in holy daring to the service of Jesus Christ, through readings these extracts.

In her own words, *'I believe that religion is all or nothing. God is either first or He is nowhere with us individually. The very essence and core of religion is 'God first', and allegiance and obedience to Him first.'*

God be with you.

Catherine Bramwell-Booth

Prepared by Commissioner Catherine Bramwell-Booth (R) just five months prior to her promotion to Glory on 3 October, 1987, at the advanced age of 104 years.

THE CHRIST OF GOD

The Christ of God was a real veritable person, who walked about, and taught, and communicated with men; who helped and saved them from their evil appetites and passions, and who promised to keep on doing so to the end of the world; who called his followers to come out from the evil and sin of the world to follow him, carrying his cross, obeying his words, and consecrating themselves to the same purposes for which he lived and died.

He never undertook to be true instead of me, but to make me true to the very core of my soul. He never undertook to make me pass for pure, either to God or man, but to enable me to *be* pure. He never undertook to make me pass for honest and sincere, but to renew me in the spirit of my mind so that I could not help but be both, as the result of the operation of his Spirit within me. He never undertook to love God instead of my doing so with *'all my heart and mind and soul and strength'*, but he came on purpose to empower and inspire me to do this.

The Word was made flesh, and dwelt among us, (and we beheld his glory, the glory as of the only begotten of the Father,) full of grace and truth.
JOHN 1:14

11

BREAD OF LIFE

Let me try to put before you what I conceive to be the true representation of the Christ of God. We say that he meets the whole world's need - that he comes to it walking on the waves of its difficulties, sins and sorrows, and says, *'I am the bread of life; take me, appropriate me, live by me, and you will live forever. I will resuscitate and pardon, cleanse and energise you; I am the Christ, the Saviour of the world.'* This is the divine word, or deliverer, which philosophers have longed for, and stretched out their hands to embrace.

Man needed some being outside himself, above him, and yet able to understand and pity him in his utmost guilt, misery, and helplessness - able to inspire him with *a new life*, to impart light, love, strength, and endurance, and to do this always and everywhere, in every hour of darkness, temptation, and danger.

Humanity needed an exhibition of God, not merely to know that he was an almighty Creator, but that he is a pitiful Father, yearning and waiting to save him. God's expedient for showing this to man was to come in the flesh.

How otherwise could God have revealed himself to fallen man?

Jesus said unto them, I am the bread of life: he that cometh to me shall never hunger; and he that believeth on me shall never thirst.
JOHN 6:35

ABBA, FATHER!

We make all of Christ, only it is a living Christ instead of a dead one. It is Christ in us, as well as for us, Christ in us - an ever-loving, ever-present, almighty Saviour - is just able to do what the angels said he should do, that for which he was called Jesus, *viz.* to save his people from their sin.

Then how does he do this? Wherein does he supercede the law? Wherein does Christ do for me and wherein is he made to me, what the law could not do or be to me?

We have seen that the law fails just at the point of power. Now, how does Christ become this power to me? How is he made unto me wisdom, righteousness, sanctification and redemption? How does he save us from the power of sin?

He does it first by giving *assurance of salvation.* He saves and then he makes us conscious of the fact, which the law could not do. All it could do was to set us struggling after it. It could not give us assurance. Now, by assurance, I mean the personal realisation of my acceptance in Christ, my acceptance by the Father, my present experience. I mean the inward assurance which men and women find for themselves, or have revealed in themselves, which they know as a matter of consciousness.

It is believing in a living, personal and almighty Saviour, and believing in him now, and that faith brings realisation. When people believe thus, they have the witness of the Spirit that they are in Christ Jesus.

For as many as are led by the Spirit of God, they are the sons of God. For ye have not received the spirit of bondage again to fear; but ye have received the Spirit of adoption, whereby we cry, Abba, Father.
ROMANS 8:14,15

THE KEY

Nobody knows the soul but God. Nobody can see the secret windings of the depraved heart but God. Nobody can tell when a soul is whole-hearted but God, and as soon as he sees it he will tell that soul that it is saved. But if God has not told you, be up and stirring for you are not saved yet, or you would know it.

What are you to believe unto? Hope? No! you don't believe unto hope. Effort? No! you had that before in the law. Salvation? Yes! and if you *'believe unto salvation'*, you will get saved, and if you are not saved, you have never believed unto salvation. Instead of trying to make yourself happy in this state of uncertainty and misery, for Christ's sake get up and get saved. It is a great deal easier to get saved than it is to make yourself believe you are saved when you are not.

The one is a philosophical impossibility, the other is a glorious possibility at any moment when you get low before God and give up all, and take his Son as your Saviour. God's gospel is beautifully adjusted to the laws of our mental constitution. He who wrote, framed, and conceived it, created us, and he made it like a key to fit the lock, and knows just the conditions that are necessary, and he has conformed his gospel to those conditions.

For I am not ashamed of the gospel of Christ: for it is the power of God unto salvation to every one that believeth.
ROMANS 1:16

TRUSTING

The mind is too often occupied with the theory of divine truth instead of the living person whom the truth sets forth. Now, it seems clear to me that the divine testimony concerning Christ may be believed, and frequently *is* believed, without there existing a particle of saving trust in him as a *personal Saviour*. Here is the secret of so many apparently believing and devout people living in systematic disobedience to God. Their minds are convinced of the truth, and their emotions are frequently stirred by it; but they have no life, no spiritual power in them by which to resist temptation or live above the world, because their faith does not embrace a living Saviour able to save them to the uttermost, but only the truth about him.

The term faith is used in several different senses in the Scriptures, but when used to designate that act through which a soul is justified before God, and renewed by his Spirit, it always signifies trust in, or committal to, a living Saviour. The word used to signify this trust is sometimes rendered commit, as in John 2:24: *'But Jesus did not commit himself unto them, because he knew all men.'*

He did not believe in them, or *trust* them with his person - he did not commit himself into their power. This is just what God requires of the sinner to do in order to be saved - to *commit himself* to the faithfulness and power of Jesus.

But as many as received him, to them gave he power to become the sons of God, even to them that believe on his name.
JOHN 1:12

15

ADOPTION

It is evident that the scriptural idea of saving faith is that of the absolute committal of the whole being over to the faithfulness and power of Jesus, and not merely a belief, however firm, of the records of certain facts concerning him. I may believe that he is the Saviour - that he dies for me - that he intercedes for me - that he has promised to save me, as thousands do, and yet I may have no trust in him as now doing all this for me, and consequently draw no sap, no spiritual virtue, from him.

Saving faith consists in a firm trust in the person of jesus, and committal of the soul to him by an unwavering act of confidence in him for all that the Bible presents him to be, as the Redeemer and Saviour of men: *'For I know whom I have believed, and am persuaded that he is able to keep that which I have committed unto him against that day'* (2 Timothy 1:12).

As soon as this trust is exercised, the testimony of the Spirit is given to adoption, and the soul *knows* that it has passed from death unto life. Of course this trust is exercised *through* the testimony of God to his Son, but the Son is *the object of trust,* and not the testimony merely.

I know whom I have believed, and am persuaded that he is able to keep that which I have committed unto him against that day.
2 TIMOTHY 1:12

RENEWAL

What God does for us through Jesus Christ outside of us is one thing, and what he does in us by Jesus Christ is another thing, but the two are simultaneous, or one so immediately succeeds the other that we hardly discern the interval. Now, I say, I want power to enable me to meet that temptation which is coming on me tomorrow, as it came on me yesterday, but, if Jesus Christ pardons me ever so, and leaves me under the reigning power of my old appetites, what has he done for me? I shall be down in the mud and tomorrow night I shall be as condemned as ever.

I want power. I want regeneration, as the Holy Spirit has put it. I want the renewing of the spirit of my mind. I want to be created anew in Christ Jesus, *'made a new creature'*.

Therefore if any man be in Christ, he is a new creature: old things are passed away; behold, all things are become new.
2 CORINTHIANS 5:17

This is where Jesus Christ transcends the law. The law could not renew the spirit of my mind. it could only show me what a guilty rebel I was. It could not put a better spirit in me, but Jesus Christ comes and does this for me - gives me power. How?

It is by the *union of my soul with him*. You say, *'Explain it!'* We cannot explain it, but we *know* it. As Jesus said to Nicodemus; *'The wind bloweth where it listeth, and thou hearest the sound thereof, but canst not tell whence it cometh, and whither it goeth: so is everyone that is born of the Spirit.'*

United to Christ I have power to conquer, to subdue, to trample under foot those things which heretofore have been my master, and by virtue of him I retain the power, and no other way.

I am the vine, ye are the branches: He that abideth in me, and I in him, the same bringeth forth much fruit: for without me ye can do nothing.
JOHN 15:5

KNOWING GOD

The things of the Spirit are only spiritually comprehended. Hence this beautiful union cannot be explained; I only know it is spoken of all through the Bible, both in the Old Testament and the New, as *knowing God*. After God had summed up the failures of his people, he gives them a promise, and says, *'I will betroth thee unto me in righteousness for ever, and thou shalt know the Lord,'* as though that were the end of the whole matter, really and truly to know him.

When they come to that living union of the soul with him, it brings the vital sap as it were into the branch of the tree. You know what the branch is when it is broken off. It is (still) a branch. It retains the form of a branch; and for a while the beauty and greenness of a branch, but it is broken off. There is no power in it. It can never bear fruit. Why? Because the communication is cut between itself and the vine and there is no sap in its fibre. Its life is cut off.

Now you can see why a soul who has never been truly united to Christ in this living spiritual marriage cannot bear fruit unto God.

Now we have received, not the spirit of the world, but the spirit which is of God; that we might know the things that are freely given to us of God.
1 CORINTHIANS 2:12

NEW BIRTH

The new birth is necessary because Christ insists upon it as a condition of receiving us back to his Kingdom; he was the injured party and therefore it was for God to fix the terms of reconciliation and not for us. Here he has done it, he has settled the matter that no man shall enter his Kingdom unless he is born again. Men may ignore this law or rebel against it, but in so doing they must perish.

It is necessary, secondly, because of the depravity of our hearts, depravity (which) utterly unfits us for the service of God's Kingdom. That we all inherit this depravity all are agreed, and if we want proof there is indeed too much. We find many scriptural passages on this point; we are told that *'the heart of man is deceitful above all things, and desperately wicked,'* and, *'the imagination of man's heart is evil continually from his youth upward.'*

The imagination of *man's* heart - not some particular class of men, but *man as such*.

The whole gospel scheme goes on the supposition that the race is depraved, destitute of all true goodness. If the heart of man were not depraved we should not have needed this system of regeneration, we should not have needed a Saviour's blood to wash out its stains and procure the power of the Holy Ghost in order that it might prosecute a holy life.

Marvel not that I said unto thee, Ye must be born again.
JOHN 3:7

NEW HEART

The Kingdom of Jesus Christ was a moral and not a physical one; he aspired to a Kingdom of the *heart*. If he had wanted a physical kingdom he could have had that without wandering up and down, *'a man of sorrows, acquainted with grief'*. He could have had that without shedding his blood on Calvary but he wanted to reign over hearts; he wanted a moral, a spiritual kingdom. He wanted a little paradise on earth and to procure that he had to shed his heart's blood. He came to win men's *hearts* back to God, and if he has not done that he has done nothing.

It is only those who have been regenerated by the Holy Ghost and whose hearts are in submission to and harmony with him who belong to his Kingdom - wherein there is no rebellion and where subjects are always in obedience. They serve because they love, not because they are forced.

A new heart also will I give you, and a new spirit will I put within you: and I will take away the stony heart out of your flesh, and I will give you an heart of flesh.
EZEKIEL 36:26

NEW LIFE

Let us try to find out what the Saviour intended by this new birth. Evidently he meant the beginning of true spiritual life in the soul. He intimates that so great a change must take place in our souls as could only be illustrated by the great change which takes place in our bodies at our natural birth. I want you carefully to mark the terms used by the Saviour here, and also the figure. By the terms used our Lord evidently signifies an *alteration* or change passing upon something which *before existed*.

The soul existed before, but it is to be regenerated by the Holy Ghost. Again, this change is spoken of as being *'renewed in the spirit of our minds'*. The same idea, you see - that what previously existed shall be renewed, transformed, and changed in character. This new birth is a renewal of the old soul, making the man himself a new creature in Christ Jesus; hence the figure used by our Lord truly illustrates his meaning, seeing that the natural birth is not a new creation, but the introduction of something previously created into a new life.

Just so, the soul, when it is born again, is introduced into a new life, into new relations with God and man, new duties, new obligations, new responsibilities, a new world!

Verily, verily, I say unto thee, Except a man be born again, he cannot see the kingdom of God.
JOHN 3:3

THE GOSPEL

What is the gospel? It is the news of the free, measureless, undeserved, reconciling mercy of God, offered to me through the vicarious, infinite, glorious sacrifice of his Son, to the end that I may be saved from sin here and from Hell hereafter! It is the news of a definite, practical end, involving conditions - for even good news to me involves certain conditions on my part, if I am to procure the good the news brings.

Therefore, I take the gospel to be aiming not merely at saving, but *restoring* us. If it were merely to save me without restoring me, what would it do for me? As a moral agent, if the gospel fails to put me right it will fail eternally to make me happy. If you were to transplant me before the throne, and put me down in the inner circle of archangels with a sense of wrong in my heart, being morally out of harmony with the laws of God and the moral laws of the universe, I should be as miserable as if I were in Hell, and should want to get away.

I must be *made right,* as well as treated as if I were right. I must be changed as well as justified. This is the gospel put as clearly in our text as it could be.

I am Jesus ... I send thee, To open their eyes, and to turn them from darkness to light, and from the power of Satan unto God, that they might receive forgiveness of sins, and inheritance among them which are sanctified by faith that is in me.
ACTS 26:15-18

THE NEW MAN

Salvation implies restoration. Salvation to a man who is sick means restoration to health; to a man dying, restoration to life; to a man on the verge of bankruptcy it means liquidation of his debts and restoration to solvency.

The common sense of mankind has prevented theoretical deliverance or mock salvation for these temporal maladies and destructions, but our great adversary, who lieth in wait to deceive, has succeeded in deluding men and women as to the reality of salvation when applied to the soul. But the salvation of God is no less real and practical for the soul than any of these temporal salvations are for the body or the circumstances.

What is man's disease? Sin, badness, falseness, spiritual death. Salvation means restoration to goodness, to truth, to spiritual life, and to God. It means deliverance from inward evil, and renewal of the heart in righteousness and true holiness. It means the right adjustment of the faculties of the soul, bringing it into harmony with the laws of its own being, with the laws of God, and with the rightful claims of its fellow beings.

In short, it means being *put right* in all its relations for time and for eternity.

Put on the new man, which after God is created in righteousness and true holiness.
EPHESIANS 4:24

PRESERVATION

Salvation means preservation. In order to preserve the well-being and happiness of a being who has been saved from any disaster or death, there must be a provision for his continuance in a state of health and safety. It would be a small mercy to save a man from drowning if he were under the cruel necessity of throwing himself into the water again tomorrow; and equally small would be the mercy of pardoning a sinner, and restoring him to a sense of peace and purity, if no provision had been made for his continuance in such a state of salvation.

The salvation of God contemplates all the weaknesses and necessities of fallen human nature, hence the Christ of God becomes *'the author of eternal salvation to all them that obey him'*. He not only restores, but he promises to dwell *in* his people as the power of an endless life, enabling them to purify their hearts by faith, to love God with all their soul and strength, and to offer themselves as living sacrifices, holy and acceptable in his sight.

He promises to empower them to resist the devil, to keep themselves unspotted from the world, and to fight manfully under the banner of his cross till death.

Though he were a Son, yet learned he obedience by the things which he suffered; and being made perfect, he became the author of eternal salvation unto all them that obey him.
HEBREWS 5:8,9

GLORIFICATION

The salvation of God embraces also glorification. How do we know? Well, first, reasoning from analogy, and seeing that the great change wrought in true saints is in the soul, and that it manifests itself in spiritual and heavenly instincts, dispositions, and aspirations, which do not find their full development or satisfaction in this life, we conclude that there is a future and more congenial sphere for such development and satisfaction.

Secondly, we have the most satisfactory evidence which mortals can give of future glorification in the fact that many are glorified before our eyes in death. Amidst the humiliation, pains, and agonies of physical dissolution, we see the soul emerging from the wreck of its physical environment, triumphing over him who hath the power of death, and in regal majesty pluming its wings for its final flight, and in view of such a victory, human reason, no less than divine revelation, declares: *'Death is swallowed up in victory.'*

For our conversation is in heaven; from whence also we look for the Saviour, the Lord Jesus Christ: who shall change our vile body, that it may be fashioned like unto his glorious body, according to the working whereby he is able even to subdue all things unto himself.
PHILIPPIANS 3:20-21

ASSURANCE

I want you to mark well that assurance of salvation is the testimony of God's spirit to a fact which has transpired, and if that fact has not transpired, God's Spirit will not testify to it.

Oh! what power assurance of salvation gives when the individual can say *'I know'*; not merely, *'I believe'*, but, *'I know'*.

St. John seems to have written his first epistle mainly to enable the believers to know: and then several times shows how we may know we are saved. Faith is the means to assurance, but assurance is not faith, and faith is not assurance. Assurance is the *result* of faith, and when you have the right sort of faith you will have assurance. *'He that believeth hath the witness in himself.'*

Until you get assurance do not trust yourself. Persevere until you get it. God will never leave a sincere soul in the dark. You must come down to the foot of the cross in the little children's way - give up all for Christ and make up your mind that you will follow him at all costs, and as soon as you do this, God *will* send the answer of his Spirit.

And this is the record, that God hath given to us eternal life, and this life is in his Son.
1 JOHN 5:11

27

PURE IN HEART

The true service of God is obedience prompted by love. *'If ye love me, keep my commandments.' 'Why call ye me, Lord, Lord, and do not the things that I say?' 'The first and greatest commandment is this: Thou shalt love the Lord thy God with all thy heart.'* How can a man love God when his heart is estranged, and full of sin and rebellion and selfishness? Impossible!

You hear the Bible and your conscience calling on you to love God. You feel that you ought, and perhaps you have tried, but you cannot. Your heart *will* love the world, pleasure, sin, business, anything but God. The moment you turn your thoughts towards God, instead of love and desire there springs up repugnance and dread. Why is this? Because your heart is wicked and therefore it is contrary to its evil nature to love God. Before you can love him, your wicked heart must be changed. And this is the reason why you cannot enter his Kingdom except you be born again.

Sinners don't understand and cannot appreciate the joys of the spiritual Kingdom; they are spiritually discerned; to the natural man they are foolishness, he cannot know them.

One of the chief of these enjoyments is knowing and loving God. To the wicked the very thought of God is misery. But the pure in heart see him, have fellowship with him, and rejoice in the light of his countenance.

Elect according to the foreknowledge of God the Father, through sanctification of the Spirit, unto obedience and sprinkling of the blood of Jesus Christ.
I PETER 1:2

INTERPRETATION

We ought to study this Book as a whole, especially the writings of the apostle (Paul). And surely we should take that which is plain and unmistakable as a key to unlock and interpret that which at first sight is difficult and contradictory. Is it not this principle which prevails in all rightly constituted human courts? Are not all human documents judged and disposed of according to this rule? Is it not insisted that these shall be interpreted consistently with themselves and with the general scope and design of the writer?

You say, 'Yes, and that is the only rational rule of interpretation.' If you were interested in a will which was in dispute, you would have a keen appreciation of the importance of this rule. Then, if this is necessary with respect to the writings of men of comparatively recent date, how much more is it necessary with repect to the writings of God - many of them having come down to us from ages back, and notwithstanding all the care that has been taken in their preservation, subject to many changes of phraseology, thus requiring in difficult passages the utmost care and skill, and yet not so much skill as *honesty*, in order to understand their meaning?

The gospel of God, (which he had promised afore by his prophets in the holy scriptures).
ROMANS 1:1,2

REALISATION

There is very little in the word of God which practically affects our salvation which is hard to be understood. The things that Paul wrote on this subject are plain enough, thank God; and this text is one of the *plainest* and most *unmistakable* in the whole Bible. Moreover, it is complete in itself, and it enunciates a great truth which underlies all God's dealings with our race.

It shows most blessedly that aback of all this apostle's reasoning about Jews and Gentiles - the predestination of the former to special privileges, and then to special judgments for the abuse of them - that aback of all this he had deep down in his soul the belief and realisation of this blessed and glorious truth, *that all God's dealings with our race are merciful and restorative,* and that in the case of the very worst of men God is doing all he can for their salvation.

He in no single instance consigns to wrath before he has truly and honestly tried to save.

The everlasting gospel to preach unto them that dwell on the earth, and to every nation, and kindred, and tongue, and people.
REVELATION 14:6

DOUBTERS

Faith is, all through the Scriptures, presented as a voluntary thing. Here is encouragement for intellectual doubters. I have met with some sincere and honest souls in my life who have been tormented almost out of their minds by intellectual doubts, yet whose hearts have been honestly inquiring after God's truth. I have a great deal more sympathy with such people than with those who profess all and do nothing.

God believes, as we do, in *honesty* and sincerity of heart; and if you have a sincere heart and want to know God, and obey him, don't be afraid that he will leave you because the devil is always shooting his hellish darts through your intellect.

Then saith he to Thomas, Reach hither thy finger, and behold my hands; and reach hither thy hand, and thrust it into my side: and be not faithless, but believing.
JOHN 20:27

Faith is a voluntary thing. It is a thing you do or leave undone, or God must have been unjust to have made a man's everlasting salvation or damnation to depend on what he has no power to do. You have *not* absolute power over your intellect, but you have *power over your heart.* You can say, *'Here, Lord, I am troubled on this subject and on that; but I am not going to wait till I can clear up all these difficulties; I will take my stand on thy declaration, and I will pledge myself to follow thee, and work thy righteousness, and do thy will, as thou shalt reveal it unto me.'*

You do that and see if God won't send you light. I know he will. He will bring you into a large place and flood your soul with his light, and those doubts, like birds of prey, will take their flight for ever, and you will know to a demonstration that *'God is light, and in him is **no darkness at all.'*** But it must be a voluntary committal of your heart to him.

But without faith it is impossible to please him: for he that cometh to God must believe that he is, and that he is a rewarder of them that diligently seek him.
HEBREWS 11:6

I COME

God wants your *heart*. Then he will enlighten your intellect. He wants you to come and take your stand alongside his throne and the cross of his Son, and commit yourself once and for ever into his hands. He wants you to say, *'Here I come with all the choice of my heart, with all the power of my will, with all the purpose of my soul - all I have and am - I come and put myself at the foot of the cross, to be yours wholly and for ever.'* I never knew a soul come to that in my life - and I have known terrible cases of conflict - who did not get flooded with light.

You see, he wants you as you want one another. When a young man woos a young woman ... what does he want? He wants *her*. He does not want to hear her say, *'I believe all you say about yourself, about your father and mother, your position and prospects.'* She may say all that, but that is not enough.

What does he want? He wants her *heart,* and that is what God wants - your heart. You may bring him your gifts, and your head-faith, and your church creeds, and your formal services, or whatever you like, but he will not accept them, and in the day of judgment he will say, *'You never gave me your heart!'*

The sacrifices of God are a broken spirit: a broken and a contrite heart, O God, thou wilt not despise.
PSALM 51:17

RESISTANCE

Truly, man is a wonderful being - and this is not surprising when we remember that he was made originally in the image of God, mentally as well as spiritually. Although fallen, eclipsed, dwarfed, yet the outline of man's make - his faculties, capacities, possibilities - remain the same.

Man can resist all the moral forces of the universe; and it is this power which constitutes his greatness and his danger. He can resist all the persuasions and entreaties of his fellowman either to good or evil. He can resist all the power of the devil. The demoniac, the possessed with a legion, could not be kept back from Jesus when he will go to him - and we are exhorted to *resist* the devil, implying, of course, that we have the power to do so.

God created man with this power, and he will not invade or ignore it. He saw it best on the whole to make men free, even though he would abuse his freedom, rather than to make him a slave, being bound to a certain result by the law of cause and effect, as the sun and stars or the animals , and consequently having no power of virtue himself, nor of bringing moral glory to his Maker.

God retains his power over man as sovereign, not by coercing his will, but by rewarding or punishing him according to the use he makes of his freedom - according to his *willing* and *acting*.

Humble yourselves therefore under the mighty hand of God, that he may exalt you in due time.
1 PETER 5:6

CHOICE

God reigns over man as a free agent, and *thus only*; and there is no text in the Bible, interpreted consistently with itself and with co-relative passages, which represents God as reigning in any other way - that is, as a *moral* Governor. Hence, when he wants to influence man in any given course, he condescends to reason with him, and to offer to his consideration motives and consequences, in order to induce him to choose as he declares. God does not take him by the collar, metaphorically speaking, and drive him in a given course with his will or without it, in the same way as he drives the sun and stars along. This would be a reflection on his own wisdom in having made him a free agent at first.

God is always *consistent with himself*, and therefore he conforms all his treatment of man to the freedom of his nature; hence he *persuades* and *strives* with man by his Holy Spirit.

Come now, and let us reason together, saith the Lord: though your sins be as scarlet, they shall be as white as snow, though they be red like crimson, they shall be as wool.
ISAIAH 1:18

ASSUMPTIONS

A scheme of theology has been thrust upon mankind which implies that God must alter human nature in order to save it. I do not mean altering it in its moral quality - making it righteous instead of sinful - but altering its constitution, saving us not as men and women, having all the capacities, propensities, and affections of humanity; but that we must, so to speak, be reorganised before God can save us. If I understand the gospel, it makes no such assumption, and comes to us with no such requirements. It was *humanity that fell*, and it was *humanity* that needed to be restored. It was *man* who fell, and God proposes to restore *man, to put us right again.*

It is an indispensable condition of a moral agent's being happy that he should be *right*. If we could be transplanted before the throne of God, retaining a sense of wrong in ourselves, feeling that we were out of harmony with the laws of the universe, and with the mind and will of God, we should be as miserable as we should be in Hell, because it is not the surroundings that make people happy, but the state of their hearts.

For all have sinned, and come short of the glory of God; being justified freely by his grace through the redemption that is in Christ Jesus.
ROMANS 3:23,24.

HARMONY

How does the gospel restore us to harmony with ourselves, harmony with moral law, and harmony with God? God, as it were, comes to me, a guilty, fallen, moral agent, and says, *'I want to pardon you, to bring you back again, not only to what you were before, but a great deal in advance of that. I want to save you, but there is one thing indispensably necessary before I can do this, and that is that I shall maintain the dignity and the righteousness of my law - I must vindicate the law which you have broken before I can pardon you.'*

It is self-evident that before God can pardon and restore the sinner, he must vindicate his own law, that this was necessary in the nature of the case. I think that persons often forget this when they talk about God not requiring an atonement, as though it were *a mere personal matter* with God. They regard it as though it were an arbitrary arrangement on his part; they do not look at the nature of the case; they do not look at the surroundings, at all the issues, or they would not think that God could set at nought his law.

To pardon the transgressor at the expense of righteousness would be a greater loss than gain.

Much more then, being now justified by his blood, we shall be saved from wrath through him.
ROMANS 5:9

Now, who was there who could have offered such atonement? Man could not offer a ransom for his brother. I question if there is, in the eyes of God, any more valuable being in the universe than man. I do not know whether the angels are more valuable in the scale of being than man; the probability seems to be the other way. God created man in his own image. Man seems to have been the darling of the Deity. His delights were with him, and the whole creation sang together at his creation, and God has manifested his extraordinary love for man by redeeming him, while he has left the angels that fell to perish.

They were only finite, created beings, whereas the law which had been broken was infinite and eternal, involving infinite and eternal consequences. Therefore they were incapable of rendering an equivalent. If there had been another being in the universe capable of offering an atonement, doubtless God would have *'spared his own Son'*, but there was not, and therefore God spared him not, but allowed him to undertake the work, and the Son voluntarily gave himself a sacrifice for us, that he might redeem us from the curse of the law.

But God commendeth his love toward us, in that, while
we were yet sinners, Christ died for us.
ROMANS 5:8

THE GREAT STOOP

When we come to look into this question of atonement, does it seem as unlikely and unreasonable as some people try to make out?

I acknowledge the stupendous character of the sacrifice. I do acknowledge the wonderful stoop it was of the divine Son to undertake it. I think I appreciate his love and goodness as much as any; but I feel as if, after all, we understand (only) a little about it. We can see how natural it was, that if the Father and the Son had created this favourite being, man, and had set their hearts on him, as they evidently had, and if Satan had thought to circumvent them by tempting man from his allegiance, and working his eternal ruin - it seems no such unlikely or unreasonable thing that, as the Deity held council and united to create man, so the Deity, foreseeing his fall, should hold council and unite to redeem him.

And, as no other being was found equal to the necessity of the case, the divine Son (undertook) it, rather than this race which he had created should be lost.

Having predestinated us unto adoption of children by Jesus Christ to himself, according to the good pleasure of his will ... In whom we have redemption through his blood, the forgiveness of sins, according to the riches of his grace.
EPHESIANS 1:5,7

SUFFICIENT

Take one illustration of the necessity of a sacrifice valuable enough to appease conscience. It is a remarkable fact, and what everyone who has worked in the Lord's vineyard knows, that it is the very last thing you can get a sinner to do, to venture on the atonement, great as it is. When the Holy Ghost has opened the sinner's eyes to the enormity of sin, quickened his conscience to perceive his condition before God, it is only by the most persistent exhibition of the greatness and sufficiency of the atonement that you can get his conscience to take hold of it, and appropriate, and be pacified by it.

Oh, how wonderfully has God guarded the sanctity of his law by putting human conscience on its side! Such an awful thing does it look to the awakened conscience that the law has been broken, that it is the very last thing you can do to get the sinner to accept even the Son of God as a sufficient atonement.

I have often said, as a last resort, to sinners, *'Was not the sacrifice enough?'* They have said, *'Oh, you don't know how guilty, you don't know how bad I have been.'* I grant it all, but was not the sacrifice sufficient? Do you ever stop to think *who was the sufferer*? He was the Son of God! Is not that enough?

How much more shall the blood of Christ, who through the eternal Spirit offered himself without spot to God, purge your conscience from dead works to serve the living God?
HEBREWS 9:14

RECONCILED

Account for it how you will, there is a fear in the human conscience that, somehow or other, it is not safe for God to pardon offenders. Conscience cannot feel that he may do it consistently, with his relation as God, and we have to get conscience to comprehend that the Son has paid the ransom before the soul will venture on it. Then we can see the absolute necessity for an atonement. Who, with any due estimate of his guilt, dare presume on the pardon of God without?

Conscience must have the assurance that God can be just and yet the justifier of the ungodly. This necessity lies deep down in our own nature; even the heathen feel it, on whom revelation has never dawned, hence they offer the fruit of their body for the sin of their soul, and inflict on themselves unheard of tortures and cruelties. They feel they are transgressors, and that they need something wherewith to appease justice, and so they try to make atonement for themselves.

Sinner, the sacrifice of Christ meets your deepest need. God has looked the subject all round, and met the whole case by letting his Son, the eternal Word, offer a sacrifice which Heaven, earth, and Hell pronounce enough! Now you can safely venture your guilty soul on the virtue of that blood.

God was in Christ, reconciling the world unto himself,
not imputing their trespasses unto them.
2 CORINTHIANS 5:19

THE NARROW DOOR

I think every reader of the New Testament must have noticed two classes of passages bearing on the question of the conditions of our salvation, the one class representing it as an exceedingly easy thing to be saved, as for instance: *'And it shall come to pass that whosoever shall call upon the name of the Lord shall be saved.'* ... and so on, all of which texts represent one side, and a glorious side, of God's truth, but not the only one.

You will find in your New Testament quite as many texts, quite as relevant, quite as important, and just as much inspired as the former class, which represent it as an exceeding *difficult* thing to be saved.

Such is my text: Strive.

We find this word would bear a stronger rather than a weaker interpretation. It would bear to be interpreted, *'fight, wrestle, agonise, to enter in at the strait gate!'* Why strive if there are no difficulties? Why fight and wrestle if there are no enemies to be encountered? And why should it be written that except a man be willing to leave his father or mother, and even life itself, he cannot be - not he *is* not - but he *cannot become* the disciple of the Lord Jesus Christ?

Strive to enter in at the strait gate: for many, I say unto you, will seek to enter in, and shall not be able.
LUKE 13:24

CHRIST'S BROKEN BODY

If you take your friend's letter in order to discover his view of any question you must read it through, or else you cannot possibly judge what your friend means. It would be unfair and dishonest to read a part and then give me a theory built on that part; you must read and *judge of the whole*. Just so with the word of God. All that bears on the subject of our salvation must be read in juxtaposition. We must look at it all round and then we shall arrive at the truth.

What a mercy it is for those who are struggling after salvation to remember that there are no difficulties on God's side of the question. There might have been, and indeed there were once, difficulties against which we might have struggled all our lives, and we could never have overcome them. There was the barrier of the broken law, with its awful penalty, which we could never have removed out of the way. But when there was no eye of pity and no arm to save, his eye pitied and his own arm brought salvation. By the glorious scheme of redemption, he bridged the yawning gulf which sin had created between himself and us, by throwing across it the broken body of his Son; and now, so far as God is concerned, the way is open and easy back again to his throne and his heart.

There is nothing more to be done on his side.

Jesus said unto him, I am the way, the truth, and the life: no man cometh unto the Father, but by me.
JOHN 14:6

43

UTMOST EFFORT

There are difficulties in the way of the salvation of every human being, fitly demanding the utmost effort which he can put forth, for although on the Godward side of the cross all barriers are cleared away, on the manward side we have need to strive and wrestle and agonize to get through the crowds which still intervene.

If this be true, we can see the necessity for the exhortation to strive, to seek, to knock, to sell all, to forsake all, to leave father and mother, and life itself, in order to save the soul. What a different idea such texts give us of our share in securing our salvation to that commonly entertained in these days! Many people seem to think that all they have to do is to sit still and wait for a wave of divine influence or power, which will come and carry them into the Kingdom of God without any concern or effort of their's.

Thousands of people remain sick because they will not endure the self-denial and trouble which the regimen requires to cure them. Your heavenly Physician has never proposed to cure you without your co-operation. He has never promised anybody to do so. And even when you are cured, you are to go on doing what he wills to will and do *in you*, or you will soon fall back again.

Work out your own salvation with fear and trembling. For it is God which worketh in you both to will and to do of his good pleasure.
PHILIPPIANS 2:12,13

44

OBSTACLES

Salvation means co-operation with God all the way through, from the first ray of light till he bids you come up higher. So you see I do not profess to preach an easy gospel, or to bring you salvation without suffering and cross-bearing. I don't believe that anybody has ever found such a salvation, and I fear those who think they have will find themselves to have been utterly deceived at last. But I want to help those of you who are awakened, to strive and wrestle to overcome what your *'but'* may be.

What is you *'but'*? That which represents in your case the man's father whom he wanted to stop and bury, or the possessions of the young ruler which Jesus told him to sell, or the honour which some of his hearers preferred to the honour that cometh from God alone.

These and kindred things are the obstacles and enemies against which men have to strive and wrestle in coming to the cross.

One thing thou lackest: go thy way, sell whatsoever thou hast, and give to the poor, and thou shalt have treasure in heaven: and come, take up the cross, and follow me. And he was sad at that saying, and went away grieved: for he had great possessions.
MARK 10:21,22

REPENTANCE

What is repentance? Repentance is simply renouncing sin - turning round from darkness to light, from the power of Satan unto God. This is giving up sin in your heart, in purpose, in intention, in desire, resolving that you will give up every evil thing, and that you will do it now. Of course this involves sorrow, for how will any sane man turn himself round from a given course into another if he does not repent having taken that forbidden course?

He is like the prodigal who, when he sat in the swineyard amongst the husks and the filth, fully resolved, and at last acted. He would never have got the father's kiss, the father's welcome, if he had not started; but he went to his father honestly and said, *'I have sinned'* - which implied a great deal more in his language then than it does in ours now.

Then comes the proof of his submission, *'and am no more worthy to be called thy son; make me as one of thy hired servants.'*

Submission is the test of penitence. My child may be willing to do 150 other things, but, if he is not willing to submit on the one point of controversy, he is a rebel, and remains one until he yields.

Here is just the difference between a spurious and a real repentance.

From that time Jesus began to preach, and to say, Repent: for the kingdom of heaven is at hand.
MATTHEW 4:17

Christ Jesus came to save his people from their sins, not in them; and those who will not be saved from their sins, proved beyond a question that they are none of his. I have known many professing Christians try hard to get peace while holding to some sin, or allowing some idol, but I never knew one succeed. You may preach faith for ever to a soul thus temporising with evil, but its consequences will be too strong for your theories. You must show that soul that it can never believe till it is willing to part with evil. Not that it must save itself, but that it must be *willing to be saved from sin*.

This is the principle on which Christ dealt with the young ruler and which is insisted on again and again by Christ and his apostles. I am satisfied that thousands hear so much about faith, and so little about the conditions of faith, that they get bewildered; and instead of repenting and putting away evil, that their sins may be blotted out, they spend all their time in trying to work themselves up into a faith as unphilosophical as it is unscriptural. Consequently they fail to get peace and live in perpetual condemnation and misery. So it must ever be with those who ignore God's way and take their own.

Christ Jesus is too much in love with his Father's will to dwell with those who will not obey it; the unalterable condition of his presence and smile is doing the will of his Father.

Now when they heard this, they were pricked in their heart, and said unto Peter and to the rest of the apostles, Men and brethren, what shall we do. Then Peter said ... Repent and be baptized ...
ACTS 2:37,38

47

SUDDEN CONVERSION

I have been very much struck with the different manner in which people argue about temporal and spiritual things. In regard to the former, supposing a friend is about to adopt some mistaken course, you ply him with the best arguments you can command, and the more quickly these take effect the better you are pleased. You praise his candour and say, *'This man is not only open to conviction, but acts spontaneously upon the light he has received.'* You do not think any the worse of him because of the readiness with which he has accepted the truth, not do you for a moment imagine that he must go through a long preparatory process before he can act upon his convictions.

Why then in the religious world should the exactly similar phenomenon be doubted simply on account of its suddenness? Surely it should be even less a subject of surprise when we remember that the special operation of the Spirit of God is to convince of sin and to present the most momentous motives and sentiments that can be laid before the human mind in favour of its abandonment.

The idea, I know, that owing to its suddenness the change will not be permanent. But this is a mistake. The permanence of a conversion is not determined by the gradual process which produces it, or by the speed with which it is accomplished, but its reality.

Verily, verily, I say unto you, He that heareth my word, and believeth on him that sent me, hath everlasting life, and shall not come into condemnation; but is passed from death unto life.
JOHN 5:24

48

MILK OF THE WORD

The most important want of the babe in Christ is unquestionably congenial aliment; it needs to be fed with *'the sincere milk of the Word'*. Deprived of this, there is no chance of life, to say nothing of growth. How important, then, that the character of the ministry should be suited to the wants of a newborn soul, *'the sincere milk of the Word'*, that which is felt to be *real*.

Words without heart will chill the very life current of a young believer. It must be that which has been *tasted* and handled of the Word of life. The spiritual babe will soon pine away under mere theoretical teaching. It must be sustaining, and in order to be this the milk must be pure, unmixed with either diluting or deleterious doctrines. It must be congenial to the cravings of a spiritual appetite and capable of being assimilated by a spiritual nature. It must be direct and practical. The babe, under its teachings, must learn how to walk in all the ordinances and statutes of the Lord blameless - how to apply the principles of action laid down in his Word to the daily occurrences of life - how to resist temptation and overcome the world. And I think, without an adequate supply of such spiritual food, the first condition of its preservation and progress will not be fulfilled.

As new born babes, desire the sincere milk of the word, that ye may grow thereby.
I PETER 2:2

A LIVING BRANCH

You can be like a branch. You can get so much scriptural knowledge that you look just like a real Christian. You can get many of the feelings of a real Christian, and of the sentiments, as well as a great many of the aspirations and desires of a Christian. You can be so like a branch that nobody, but Jesus Christ, may know you are not in that true vine, and yet you have never, as the apostle says, been grafted on to the olive tree. And therefore you go on weeping and struggling and trying to perform the function of a living branch, when all the while you are a dead one.

You go on trying to bring forth fruit unto God when the one indispensable condition of fruitfulness is wanting. You have got every other condition. You may even be nailed up to the wall close to the vine, so close to the vine that nobody can detect your want of union, excepting the Gardener who comes and closely inspects you, and yet you may not have one fibre truly circulating the real spiritual sap. *Hence you have no power* - and down you go when temptation comes.

I am the true vine, and my Father is the husbandman. Every branch in me that beareth not fruit he taketh away: and every branch that beareth fruit, he purgeth it, that it may bring foth more fruit.
JOHN 15:1,2

NATURAL APPETITES

Jesus Christ, recognises the fact that we are still in the body, still in the world, and that we are open to the attacks of Satan. He knows, and has provided for the temptations of the flesh, that is, the temptations which come through our natural appetites and instincts and desires, as they came to him.

He was hungry after enduring the great temptation of the wilderness. There was no sin in being hungry. He was intensely hungry, for he had nerves, and a brain, and a heart, as we have. He was a perfect man, and he suffered all the consequences of that lengthened strain upon his nervous system, and the devil took advantage of the existence of that intensely excited condition of his body by tempting him unlawfully to gratify it. For he said, *'Command these stones that they be made bread.'* That was unlawful under the circumstances and, therefore, he said, *'Get thee behind me, Satan.'*

He would rather suffer the hunger than unlawfully gratify it, and, therefore, he did not commit sin.

I pray not that thou shouldest take them out of the world, but that thou shouldest keep them from the evil.
JOHN 17:15

OUR WEAKNESSES

It matters not how intensely excited any physical appetite may be - *that is not sin*. The more you suffer through the excitement of physical appetite, of whatever kind it may be, the more Jesus Christ sympathises with you, for he was tempted in all points, like as we are, yet without sin.

And if you endure temptation, he will sympathise with you more than the man who does not have to endure and resist. You do not sin because of the appetite merely being excited. I think Satan gets some sincere souls to bring themselves into condemnation when God does not condemn them.

For we have not an high priest which cannot be touched with the feeling of our infirmities, but was in all points tempted like as we are, yet without sin.
HEBREWS 4:15

THE PINNACLE

Jesus Christ knows that we are susceptible to the liking of nice things like other people, and great things, and ambitious schemes, and the world's praises and censures. God's people are only too sadly familiar with this, and the weak part of their nature would respond to it and they would fall. But now they are united to Christ he opens their eyes to see that it is Satan and the world.

When the devil takes them up to the top of the pinnacle, and shows them all the glory of the world, he tries to make them think it would be nice to have it; he tempts them to think it hard that they should be regarded as such paltry and mean people, because they belong to Christ. But when they are thoroughly and truly united to Jesus, he gives them power to say, as he did, *'Get thee behind me, Satan'*, for it is written, *'Thou shalt worship the Lord thy God, and **him only** shalt thou serve'* - not him *and* the world.

Oh! thank God if you have got there. Praise the Lord if you understand that.

It is written, Thou shalt worship the Lord thy God, and him only shalt thou serve.
MATTHEW 4:10

PRESUMPTION

When the devil is foiled at all these points, he tries higher ground, *'Really you are a wonderful Christian. You have had special grace, for surely very few people can have resisted the amount of temptation you have. Really you must be one of God's specially favoured ones. Now cast yourself down. It is written, 'He shall give his angels charge concerning you.''*

Spiritual presumption next. When he is foiled through the world, and the flesh, and the devil, he then removes his old robe and comes as an angel of light. but the soul's bridegroom is hard by, and he says, *'Be not ignorant of Satan's devices. Behold I am thy salvation. Trust and be not afraid.'*

And so the soul refuses to cast itself into unnecessary troubles and is content to abide in and walk with its Lord. That is how he gives us the victory. He shows us Satan's devices, and gives us power. He said, *'I will give you power over the power of the enemy.'* This is the deliverance of the saints. This is the life of the saints. This is the fight of faith. This is the joy of salvation.

Be sober, be vigilant; because your adversary the devil, as a roaring lion, walketh about, seeking whom he may devour: Whom resist stedfast in the faith ...
I PETER 5:8,9

I have often tried to picture to myself that astounding miracle of sin, the crucifixion of the Son of God. I have gathered myself, in imagination, amongst that crowd; I have cowered down by the side of Mary, his mother; I have watched the surging crowd which was mocking him; I have seen the soldier passing up the vinegar, and looked, as it were, into the dying eyes of the Son of God.

The attempt to realise the scene has always reminded me of the saying of the Apocalypse that there was *'silence in Heaven for the space of half an hour'*.

I have always felt as though there must have been silence then, as though every heart and every voice of the Celestial City had been hushed, and as though all the inhabitants of the glorious New Jerusalem were standing looking over its battlements, and watching that dying sufferer. And I have always felt that there must have been silence in Hell itself. As if the shock of the dying of the Son of God must have reverberated to the very deepest caverns of the bottomless pit, and shaken Hell to its centre.

Heaven and Hell had sat watching that event and wondered what would be the ultimate result. It was only earth - only poor, fallen, darkened man - who could afford to pass the ribald joke, and scorn the suffering Son of God; neither angels nor devils could do either one or the other.

When he had opened the seventh seal, there was
silence in heaven about the space of half an hour.
REVELATION 8:1

TAKING SIDES

What a sight it must have been as he who was the embodiment of his Father's glory and the express image of his person - the very personification of the righteousness of his character and the righteousness of his law - hung between earth and Heaven dying as a sacrifice for the sons of men. Don't you wish you could have seen it?

Perhaps you would have been among the crowd of mockers; or you might have been among those who were trying to make a penny by casting lots for his coat; or you might have been among the Roman soldiers; or you might have been, like Nicodemus, hiding back in the crowd; or you *might* have been like the few - two or three feeble women - who stuck to him to the last.

What you are now, you would have been then. Where are you now when the Son of man is crucified? Where are you now when the interests of truth, righteousness, benevolence, and holiness, are trembling in the balance? Have you courage, now, to stand up for right? If not, you would not have had it then, for *'he that is faithful in little will be faithful in much.'*

Are you today for Jesus or Barabbas?

Whether of the twain will ye that I release unto you?
They said, Barabbas.
MATTHEW 27:21

56

RULING PRINCIPLE

On what principle did it (the world) cry out for Barabbas instead of Jesus? He was confessed by his enemies to be a good man. He had done them many good turns. He had healed their sick, and cleansed their lepers, and fed their hungry ones, and borne their sorrows and their sicknesses, even his enemies being the witnesses; and, here, Barabbas was a robber and murderer. On what principle did they cry out, *'Not this man, but Barabbas?'*

On the most natural of principles - that which influences us all - that which is the ruling principle in every man's mind, be he good or evil. The world made its selection on the ruling principle of human nature - fraternity. Barabbas was its *own.* Jesus ... was of another world. His spirit and the world's spirit were antagonistic.

Yes, the world knows whom to hate. It never makes a mistake in its selection. It knows who are not of it. If you are of the world you have nothing to fear from the world. If you are not of it, look out! It will do all the despite it can. The sin of the good in the eyes of the world is simply being good. The world's attitude toward holiness - toward goodness - has been all the way down through life that of antagonism, of opposition. It hates goodness. No matter how many good works a holy being may do, he is none the better for that in its eye because it is holiness that is the sin.

What shall I do then with Jesus which is called Christ?
They all say unto him, Let him be crucified.
MATTHEW 27:22

57

VALUES

Do you love righteousness? I do not mean in the abstract. I suppose the devil does that, at least he admires it. I do not think God has made a single intelligence that does not admire righteousness in somebody else. But do you love righteousness in the essence of it? When it clashes with your own interests? In those people round about you whose very presence is a reproof to you?

Do you say, *'Barabbas rather than this man. I cannot stand his eye, it is too keen. I cannot stand his face, it is too clear in its reproof and rebuke of iniquity. I cannot come up to his standard, it is too high?'* Do you love righteousness in its bearings upon yourself? Do you love it in aspiring after it, in being willing to sacrifice for it, in desiring it above anything on earth, or in Heaven?

If you do, then you are on the side of Jesus Christ. If not, you are crying, *'Barabbas'* , just as truly as if you had stood with the mocking crowd. If you do not love righteouness, and if you do not love the most righteous, godly people on earth, better than you love your own sister after the flesh, then you have not the Spirit of Jesus in you, and would have cried, *'Barabbas'*.

Except your righteousness shall exceed the righteous-
nees of the scribes and Pharisees, ye shall in no case
enter into the kingdom of heaven.
MATTHEW 5:20

FOR YOU

Saviours must be sufferers. Jesus was counted among the transgressors. He was not a transgressor, for he was the very embodiment of his Father's law, but they made him a transgressor. He was a technical transgressor! He transgressed their technicalities; he broke their Sabbath, but he did not break his Father's Sabbath. He said he was a king, and they made him a traitor, and made it out that he was an enemy of Caesar, but he did not sin in God's estimation. He was the very embodiment of righteousness, yet he was numbered amongst the transgressors. What for? For you and me.

It was necessary that he should personify the transgressor in order to save the transgressor. It was necessary that he should die under the penalty of the technical law in order that he might help to fulfil the everlasting law of righteousness and benevolence. He did it. Will you follow him or will you stick by the technical and sacrifice the spiritual righteousness?

The difference between the Son of God and the Pharisees who helped to accuse him was that he always carried out the spirit of his Father's law; they carried out the letter - when it suited them. Do you so love righteousness that you dare to go and rescue the victims of unrighteousness? There is abundant opportunity for trying yourself.

Jesus answered ... My Father worketh hitherto, and I work. Therefore the Jews sought the more to kill him, because he not only had broken the sabbath, but said also that God was his Father, making himself equal with God.
JOHN 5:17,18

Do you see? Human condemnation and condemnation at human tribunals is no evidence in itself against the righteous sufferer, nor is it any sign of the displeasure of God, otherwise he would have sent his own Son to everlasting ignominy.

Jesus said, *'It is a small thing that we should be judged of man's judgment.'* It is a small thing that we should be dragged up before human tribunals if our own conscience condemn us not. Thank God human tribunals will be swept away by-and-by. At the last great day they will stand there side by side - judges, juries and magistrates - side by side with the criminals. There will be no mistakes. The wrong man will never get to the wrong side there; and the Great Eternal will pronounce the sentence. Are you ready for that?

The greatest human disgrace and suffering for righteousness' sake are a prelude to the highest honour and the most undying glory. Hold on, my persecuted brethren. For those who are persecuted for righteousness' sake, it will be well by-and-by.

Note, finally, this Man's name, of whom they said, *'Not this man, but Barabbas.'* This Man's name has ever since that day been above every name. The eternal decree has gone forth that this Man's yoke every neck shall wear, and to his rod everyone shall bow, and that the great song in the New Jerusalem shall be, *'Glory, honour, and power be unto'* - whom? - *'Unto him that was slain!'*

Blessed are they which are persecuted for righteousness' sake: for their's is the kingdom of heaven.
MATTHEW 5:10

THE COMPASSION

The compassion of Jesus stands out distinguished as of another kind by its clear perception of the worst features of man's condition.

No doubt the Saviour's heart ached in sympathy with the mass of human sorrow, sickness, and poverty brought before him. Where we have only a glimpse of man's troubles as we move hurriedly up and down among them, he had the whole sad story unfolded to him, and his keen love responded tenderly to every cry for help.

Nevertheless he was never diverted from the *great central danger*. To him the sorrowful troubled crowd were not merely poor and suffering, not merely oppressed by unjust laws, and crowded into badly constructed dwellings; not merely hungry, hard-worked, and comfortless; these were incidents which he sometimes alleviated and more often shared, but the crowning peril, the absolutely certain woe which eclipsed, in his sight, every other was the loss of the soul. He flings aside contemptuously the thought that living well in this world was a real benefit.

'For what shall it profit a man, if he shall gain the whole world and lose his own soul? Or what shall a man give in exchange for his soul?' may be taken as indicating the foundation principle of his entire scheme of redemption.

For what shall it profit a man, if he shall gain the whole world, and lose his own soul? Or what shall a man give in exchange for his soul?
MARK 8:36,37

FRIENDS

Christ's compassion stands out in its spiritual fellowship. The King of kings makes eternal friends of the fishermen. He did not visit the poor, having his fellowship, his joys, his sorrows apart from them, but he shared his life with them in a holy comradeship. He did not live in the style and companionship of the worldly Pharisees and occasionally visit Peter, James and John, and hold meetings for the working classes; no, he lived with them and became education, elevation, salvation, and all to them by his blessed fellowship. His heart had no reserves for these men.

That they could not always understand him was their fault, not his, but their slowness and dullness never wearied his compassion, nor caused him to seek friends elsewhere. He called his three fishermen to him when he was about to put forth any wonderful exercise of power. He wanted Peter, James and John when he was raising the dead, and took them to share his joy on the mount of transfiguration. He craved for their presence in his last agony and desired no better provision for his mother, when he hung upon the cross, than the home that one of them could afford.

I have called you friends; for all things that I have heard of my Father I have made known unto you.
JOHN 15:15

HOPE

The compassion of Jesus is yet further distinguished by its divine faith, and hope, and action. He had faith in the possibilities of these people, which possibilities would not have been apparent to any other eye. He believed in the transforming power of the Spirit which he could send them.

His hope was not chilled by stupidity, or foolishness, or non-comprehension on the part of the disciples.

Mighty compassion must have been that could live thirty years on such terms with such man and never falter or turn back ... Christ hoped all things, believed all things, until the Peter who was afraid of a servant girl stood triumphant before the 3,000 converts. Christ kept his little band together although he knew there was a traitor amongst them - the traitor who would betray him, and sell him for money into the hands of his enemies. Christ forbore and worked with John until the man who wanted to call fire from Heaven to burn up sinners became the apostle of love.

Christ went up to Calvary undismayed by his perfect knowledge of sinful, perverse, opposing men, to die for the whole ungrateful race. Talk about eternal hope! Is not this the eternal hope which saves to the uttermost now and here?

As many as received him, to them gave he power to become ...
JOHN 1:12

INVISIBLE KINGDOM

The compassion of Jesus is distinguished by his ever going straight to the one end. The whole work of Christ was aimed at the salvation of men's souls. And this is not the less true because he also benefited their bodies by healing their diseases and sympathising with their sorrows.

This latter side of his work is much dwelt upon and yet it was a merely incidental part. If he had come to remove earthly suffering, poverty, oppression, and distress, he would certainly have gone about it in a different way. He would have aimed at riches and position and ease in order that he might have shared them with his chosen ones. He would have sought to build up an earthly kingdom where men should neither hunger, nor thirst, nor be sick, nor die; and it would have been a far easier task than the founding of that new invisible Kingdom where only the spiritual and eternal should be of importance.

In comparison, how much easier to have drawn crowds if he had always given them their dinner than to hold followers who should enter into the mysterious doctrine, *'I am the bread of life'* (and) *'Ye must be born again.'*

Verily, verily, I say unto you, Ye seek me, not because ye saw the miracles, but because ye did eat of the loaves, and were filled.
JOHN 6:26,27

OVERFLOWING

Charity is divine, (and) springs only where the plough-share of true repentance has broken up the fallow ground of the heart, and where faith in the crucified Saviour has purified it, and where the blessed Holy Spirit has taken permanent possession. It is the love *of* God - not only love *to* God, but *like* God, *from* God, and fixed on the same objects and ends which he loves. It is a divine implantation by the Holy Ghost.

Perhaps you are saying, *'Then it is useless for me to try to cultivate it because I have not got it.'* Exactly! You may cut and prune and water for ever, but you can never cultivate that which is not planted; your first work is to *get this love* shed abroad in your heart.

It is one of the delusions of this age that human nature only wants pruning, improving, developing, and it will come out right. No, no! If you want this divine love you must break up the fallow ground of your hearts and invite the heavenly husbandman to come and sow it - shed it abroad in your soul.

The love of God is shed abroad in our hearts by the Holy Ghost which is given unto us.
ROMANS 5:5

THE TRUTH IN LOVE

Divine charity is not only consistent with but very often necessitates reproof and rebuke on the part of its possessor. It renders it incumbent on those who possess it to reprove and rebuke whatever is evil - whatever does not tend to the highest interests of its object.

This charity conforms in this, as in everything else, to its divine model: *'As many as I love, I rebuke and chasten'* - when necessary for the good of its object. We will just turn to a beautiful illustration of the working of this divine charity in the heart and life of the apostle who wrote 1 Corinthians 13 ...

'But when Peter was come to Antioch, I withstood him to the face, because he was to be blamed. For before that certain came from James, he did eat with the Gentiles: but when they were come, he withdrew and separated himself, fearing them which were of the circumcision. And the other Jews dissembled likewise with him; insomuch that Barnabus also was carried away with their dissimulation. But when I saw that they walked not uprightly according to the truth of the gospel, I said unto Peter before them all ...' Galations 2:11-15.

Well done, Paul! Noble, glorious, courageous charity that!

Speaking the truth in love, may grow up into him in all things, which is the head, even Christ.
EPHESIANS 4:15

REBUKE

Our Lord whose whole soul was love, whose life was one sacrifice for the good of his creatures, faithfully rebuked even his own when they erred from the truth, and how fearlessly he exposed and denounced the shallowness and hypocrisy of those who professed to love God, and yet contradicted this profession in their lives. How fearlessly he reproved sin everywhere.

He said to his disciples on one ocassion, *'Ye know not what manner of spirit ye are of. For the Son of man is not come to destroy men's lives, but to save them.'* As if he had said, *'You ought to have learned this before now.'*

Oh that your charity and mine might not lack this lineament of divine likeness. Would to God there were more of this faithful, loving charity that dares to reprove sin, and to rebuke its brother, instead of false charity that fawns on a man to his face and goes behind him and stabs him in the back.

He drove them out of the temple ... and said unto them that sold doves, Take these things hence; make not my Father's house an house of merchandise. And his disciples remembered that it was written, The zeal of thine house hath eaten me up.
JOHN 2:15-17

ACTION

What a contrast between Saul (of Tarsus) and Paul. Did you ever think about it? What does he say? *'I went about to establish my own righteousness.'* That was his inspiring motive; that was the spring of his action before he got true charity; not that he cared for the Kingdom of God, but he cared for his own honour, glory and exaltation, and wanted to stand well with his nation. Then contrast him when he becomes Paul. What does he say? *'For I could wish that myself were accursed from Christ for my brethren, my kinsmen according to the flesh.'* There is charity, if you like.

There is a contrast. He does not care now what they think of *him*. Self is lost sight of altogether now. Paul's heart and soul and efforts are set on the salvation of men. If they choose to praise him, he takes it as a matter of course; if they choose to condemn him, he takes that as a matter of course too. It is not Paul now; it is Christ and his Kindom.

I live; yet not I, but Christ liveth in me.
GALATIANS 2:20

CONFLICT

Divine charity often involves conflict. It was so with our Lord. He was the very personification of it. He was love itself and grace and truth poured from his lips incessantly. His blessed feet went about doing good and his hands ministered to the necessities and happiness of his creatures, yet his whole course was one of conflict, opposition, and persecution. His proper mission was to bring peace on earth, but the result of it was a sword. Why? It was not his fault. He would doubtless have liked to have *'lived peaceably with all men'* for he was the Prince of peace.

Then how was it that wherever he went there was a sword, opposition, and conflict to the death? Why? Because men resisted and rejected his divine and heavenly ministrations. They would not have his rebukes and his teaching because they (were) condemned (by) them. They would not listen to his voice and therefore they went about to persecute him and to kill him.

If it is possible, as much as lieth in you, live peaceably with all men.
ROMANS 12:18

REPROACH

Look out! God has wonderful ways of chastising his people in those very things in which they sell his interest. But you say that everything will be against you. Yes, very likely. Let us settle that at once. Let none of these things move you. You say, *'It will be a life of conflict to the end.'* Very likely, so was his. *'I am weak,'* you say. He knows all about that. You say, *'It will be cutting to have people saying this and saying the other.'* I know it is cutting but that is the path he calls you to tread and he will give you grace to bear the cutting.

'Blessed are ye, when men shall revile you, and persecute you, and shall say all manner of evil against you falsely, for my sake.'

He does not show where he is leading us, so we can only go a step at a time. The future may look dark, but let us be fully persuaded in our minds that the step in advance is the step the Lord wants us to take - then take it, and leave the future with him. Come out, as Abraham did, not knowing whither you go; and, as sure as he sits on the throne, the very things that you sacrifice, or that you think you sacrifice, for him, he will give you as a reward of your faithfulness.

If ye be reproached for the name of Christ, happy are ye; for the spirit of glory and of God resteth upon you: on their part he is evil spoken of, but on your part he is glorified.
1 PETER 4:14

SORROWING LOVE

True charity sticks to the Lord Jesus (even) when he is fainting under his cross, as well as when the people are cutting down the boughs and crying, *'Hosanna!'*

I often think if times of persecution were to come again, how many of us would be faithful? How many would go to the dungeon? How many would stand by the truth with hooting, howling mobs at their heels, such as followed him on the way to the cross? How many of us would stick to him then? But that is the kind of love that will stand the test on the judgment day.

Have you got this charity Love in sorrow, love in suffering, love in isolation, love in persecution, love in death? Have we got this love? There is much need of it this day.

And now abideth faith, hope, charity, these three; but the greatest of these is charity. Follow after charity ...
I CORINTHIANS **13:13; 14:1**

ALONE

The possession of divine charity often necessitates walking a lonely path.

Not merely in opposition and persecution but *alone in it*, and here again, Jesus who was the personification of divine love, stands out as our great example. he was emphatically alone and of the people there was none with him. Even the disciples whom he had drawn nearest to him, and to whom he had tried to communicate most of his thought and spirit, were so behind that he often had to reprove them, and to lament their obtuseness and want of sympathy. *'Ye shall leave me alone.'*

In the greatness of his love he had to go forward into the darkness of Gethsemane. He was alone while they slept, and then he went all alone, through ribaldry, scorn, and sarcasm, to the judgment hall. He stood alone before Pilate. On the cross he hung unaccompanied! - *alone*.

It was so with Paul. *'At my first answer no man stood with me'*, and it has commonly been so with those whom God has called to extraordinary paths. Must John have a revelation of things shortly to come to pass? He must go alone into the Isle of Patmos. Must Paul hear unspeakable words, not at that time lawful for a man to utter? He must go alone into the third heaven and not be allowed even to communicate what he saw and heard when he came down.

And Enoch walked with God: and he was not; for God took him .
GENESIS 5:24
All the disciples forsook him, and fled.
MATTHEW 26:56

DIRECTION

When God has called some of his followers to an out-of-the-way path, they have had to go alone in an untrodden way. Superior love necessitates a lonely walk. You shrink and say, *'That seems so hard.'* Yes, I know; I wish I could make it easier, but I cannot help it because, you see, it is only they who thus love to whom the Lord tells his secrets. Then, when he gives to any soul superior light to its fellows, and that soul *follows* the light, it necessarily entails a path in advance of its fellows. Unless he can inspire and encourage them to follow, he must go on alone.

In Acts 10 when Peter saw that he had not yet explored all the ideas of the divine mind about the extension of his Kingdom, that his business was to follow his Lord's directions, and not have his own *'ifs'* and *'buts'*, but go ahead and do as the Lord bade him, then Peter went on to carry out the divine direction.

Then the Church - this new Church - which had only just itself been brought to God by a new Saviour, a new revelation, a new call, a new faith, is down upon Peter, and summons him before a council to answer for his conduct.

He tells them all about it in the truthful simplicity of a man of God, and, thank God, they had sense enough, yes, and love enough, to accept his explanations, and to glorify God.

And the Spirit bade me go ... nothing doubting.
ACTS 11:12

STEP OUT

It is self-evident that until the Church - I mean the people of God - have explored all the ideas which are in the divine mind for the propagation of his Kingdom in the earth, somebody must be always receiving new light and making new departures, and there has never been a single instance in the history of the Church in which this has been done, but nearly the whole generation has raised a hue and cry against it!

How would it be possible for God to bring about a revolution - a true revival - a grand aggressive movement of Christianity without giving new light and calling somebody to some path in advance of all that has gone before? And what does it matter who - whether it is Peter, or John, or Luther, or Fox, or Wesley, or Booth - what does it matter, *so that God does it?*

But this necessitates somebody *leading the way* - going on in advance. Will *you* be content to go in advance? Will *you* endure the hardness of a pioneer? Can you bear the ridicule and gibes of your fellow-men? Dare *you* go where the Holy Spirit leads, and leave him to look after the consequences? If so, happy are you, and you shall have a harvest of precious souls, but, if you draw back, his soul shall have no pleasure in you.

The Lord help you! Step out on to the divine love, that is able to make you more than a conqueror. Step out - follow, follow, follow - do not be afraid!

And a vision appeared to Paul in the night; There stood a man of Macedonia, and prayed him, saying, Come over into Macedonia, and help us.
ACTS 16:9

BY LOVE COMPELLED

True charity holds out, in spite of ingratitude, opposiiton and persecution. Its possessor takes the good of all men, not because he ought merely, but because he cannot help it. His heart is on the side of God and truth. He loves righteousness and, therefore, cannot desist from seeking to bring all beings to love it, too, although they hate and despise him for so long. Jesus held out in this glorious love even in the agonies of the crucifixion. *'Father, forgive them; they know not what they do.'* His heart was set on bringing men back to God and he went through with it. His soul did not draw back and his divine love constrained him even unto death.

Paul followed his Master in this respect; and though the more he loved some of his converts, the less he was loved, he went on, seeking their highest good, not being hindered for a moment by their ingratitude. He loved *them* - not their good opinion or applause. A spurious charity soon tires when the objects of it prove unworthy. Its possessor says, *'I have had enough of this; the kinder I am, the worse people treat me. I shall button up my pocket and take my ease, till I am better appreciated.'*

Self-glory is the very life of spurious charity: it dies right out under ingratitude and contempt.

Love your enemies, bless them that curse you, do good to them that hate you, and pray for them which despitefully use you, and persecute you.
MATTHEW 5:44

THE PROMISE

What would be the first thing that would strike you that the disciples would be thinking of as they wended their way back from Olivet, having taken leave of their now glorified Master? Back again to the upper room at Jerusalem. Imagine what state of mind would be theirs. How would they wait for the promise?

The first feeling would be of deep *self-abasement*. As they thought of the past, now that the full glory of his divinity and the divinity of his mission had burst upon them, all he would have revealed to them, if they would have received it - as the thought burst in upon them these apostles would say, indeed as he said, *'O fools, and slow of heart to believe!'*

They were cured - Peter certainly was - of self-sufficiency, of pride, and all of them would go back again in deep self-abasement.

Ye shall receive power, after that the Holy Ghost is come upon you: and ye shall be witnesses unto me both in Jerusalem, and in all Judea, and in Samaria, and unto the uttermost part of the earth.
ACTS 1:8

SOMETHING MORE

How do you think they felt when they got into the upper room? We are told that there were about 120 of them. How do you think they felt as the thought of the past, remembered the ignominious crucifixion of their Lord, looked forward to the future, and contemplated the work to which he had called them?

And what was it? It was not to go and set up an idol of Jesus Christ alongside of other idols in the temples of the heathen gods, but it was to go into the city of Jerusalem, where they had just crucified him between two thieves, and proclaim him as the long-expected Messiah of the Jews. It was to begin to set up the royal spiritual Kingdom in contra-distinction to their temporal and earthly kingdom, and they go out from Jerusalem and subjugate the world to his sway!

Poor Peter, and Thomas, and John, and Mary, and the rest of the women (thanks to the Holy Ghost, he has taken care to put it in that they were there!) - how would they feel? They would feel, *'We might as well stop and die here, as go out as we are, until we do get the equipment of power. We want something more than we have got.'*

And there they waited, and they said, *'Lord, pour it out upon us; we are ready.'* God never gave this gift to any human soul who had not come to the point that he would sell all he had to get it. Have you come to that?

Then returned they to Jerusalem from the mount called Olivet, which is from Jerusalem a sabbath day's journey. And when they were come in, they went up into an upper room ... These all continued with one accord in prayer and supplication.
ACTS 1:12-14

OBEDIENCE

They waited in *obedient faith*. How do we know? Because *they did as he bid them* - that is the evidence. Peter might have said, when he had seen his Lord off to Heaven, *'Well, what am I going to do now? I have been a long time running after the Lord in Palestine, I must betake myself to the fishing. I can wait as well on the sea beach as in Jerusalem. I wonder why the Lord told me to go to Jerusalem? I think it rather unreasonable. He might have thought of my old father and mother at home. I think I shall go back to my fishing nets.'* No, no, they had been cured of their unbelief by the last few days' experience. They had learned better than to dictate to their Master, they knew he had a good purpose in sending them to Jerusalem, and so they went there and did as he bade them - straight. Back to the upper room they went.

Mary might have said, *'I've been running and ministering to the Saviour a long time, I'm afraid my friends will think I am neglecting home duties and the claims of old friends. I really must go home and see to matters a bit; I may as well wait there for the Holy Ghost as at Jerusalem.'* No, Mary had learned better. She went back to Jerusalem. We have got their names. And they entered into the upper room and shut the door and waited - obedient faith! One of your poets said:

> Obedient faith that waits on thee,
> Thou never wilt reprove.

I send the promise of my Father upon you: but tarry ye in the city of Jerusalem, until ye be endued with power from on high.
LUKE 24:49

Remember from whence you have fallen. Reflect on what you once enjoyed. How was it with you in days gone by? Let me help you remember, by a few practical questions. Did you not once realise a sweet and blessed sense of your acceptance with God? And did not his Spirit witness with your spirit that you were a child of God? And did you not realise that *'there is therefore now no condemnation to them which are in Christ Jesus, who walk not after the flesh, but after the Spirit'*? How is it with you now? As you received the Lord Jesus, have you so walked in him that your path has been like that of the just, shining brighter and brighter unto the perfect day? Or have you lost your role, and with it your peace and joy of the Lord, which once was your strength?

Again, did you not once walk in daily communion with God, your prayers being not merely petitions, but mediums of sensible intercourse with him? What is your present experience? You once realised the power of Christ to rest upon you, so that you were more than conqueror over the world, the flesh, and the devil; sin had no more dominion over you and you could sing, *'Thanks be to God, which giveth us the victory through our Lord Jesus Christ,'* and, *'I can do all things through Christ, which strengtheneth me.'*

How is it with you?

Remember therefore from whence thou art fallen, and repent, and do the first works.
REVELATION 2:5

THE GIFT

It is as much the privilege of the youngest and weakest believer to be filled with the Spirit, as it is of the most advanced, if the believer will comply with the conditions, and conform to the injunctions of the Saviour on which he has promised this gift. I do not find two standards of Christian experience here at all. I do not believe God ever intended there should be a lower life and a higher life.

This Pentecost is offered to all believers. It comes, or it would come, in the experience of every believer, if he would have it. God wants you to have it. God calls you to it. Jesus Christ has bought it for you and you may have it and live in its power as much as these apostles did, if you will - every one of you.

My dear friends, you may have it, be filled with it, and no one but God knows what he would do with you and what he would make of you if you were thus filled, for the experience of Peter shows how utterly different a man is *before* he gets a pentecostal baptism and *after* he gets it. The man who could not stand the questionings of a servant-girl before he got this power, dared to be crucified after he got it.

John truly baptized with water; but ye shall be baptized with the Holy Ghost not may days hence.
ACTS 1:5
Be filled with the Spirit.
EPHESIANS 5:18

LORD OF ALL

My young friends, listen to the voice of the Spirit within you. Accept of no compromise between Christ and the world. You had better go back, as the young ruler did, than become a hypocrite, and lose both worlds. The condition of discipleship remains unaltered: *'If any man come to me, and hate not* (is not willing to give up if fidelity to me requires it) *his father and mother, and his own life also **he cannot be** my disciple.'*

Jesus claims from first to last to be first in your love, your interest, your service. He never pretends to claim any less, and broadly says again and again that whoever withholds this allegiance must forego all claim to his love and mercy for ever.

No man, having put his hand to the plough, and looking back is fit for the kingdom of God.
LUKE 9:62

DETERMINATION

Real Christianity is, in its very nature and essence, aggressive. We get this principle fully exhibited and illustrated in the parables of Jesus Christ. If you will study them you will find that he has not given us anything to be used merely for ourselves, but that we hold and possess every talent which he has committed to us for the good of others and for the salvation of man.

How wonderfully this principle was exhibited in the lives of the apostles and early Christians! How utterly careless they seemed to be of everything compared with this - this was the first thing with them everywhere! How Paul, at the very threshhold, counted nothing else of any consequence, but willingly, cheerfully, gave up every other consideration to live for this. And so with the early Christians, who were scattered through the persecutions - how they went everywhere preaching the word; how earnest and zealous they were. Even after the apostolic age, we learn from ecclesiastical history how they pushed themselves in everywhere; how they made converts and won real, self-denying followers, even in king's courts: how they would not be kept out, and would not be kept down, and would not be hindered or silenced.

Like their Master, they could not be hid; they could not be repressed - so aggressive, so constraining, was the spirit which inspired and urged them on.

And the lord said unto the servant, Go out into the highways and hedges, and compel them to come in, that my house may be filled.
LUKE 14:23

SUBMISSION

You say, *'Can we have this power equally with the early disciples?'* I say, reasoning from analogy, assuming that what God has done in the past he will continue to do in the future, is it not likely that he will give it to us, because we equally need it? First, *because the character of the agents is the same.* We are very much like them and they were very much like us. Thank God. It has often encouraged me. If they had been men of gigantic intellects and extraordinary education, training and position; if they had possessed all human equipment and qualifications, we might have looked back through the ages in despair, and said, *'I can never be such as they were.'*

Look what they were, naturally, apart from this gift of power. The Holy Ghost has taken care to give us their true characters. They were men of like passions, weaknesses, tendencies, liability to fall, with ourselves - just such poor, frail, weak, easily-tripped-up creatures, and, in many instances, unbelieving and disobedient, before Pentecost. Now, I say this is encouraging for us all.

Will you come and let him baptise you? Will you learn, once and for ever, that it is not a question of *human merit, strength, or deserving at all,* but simply a question of *submission, obedience, faith?*

And they were all amazed and marvelled, saying one to another, Behold, are not all these which speak Galileans? And how hear we every man in our own tongue, wherein we were born?
ACTS 2:7,8
But God hath chosen the weak things of the world to confound the things which are mighty.
1 CORINTHIANS 1:27

SUCCESS

Satan knew what was the secret of the great success of those early disciples. It was their whole-hearted devotion, their absorbing love to Christ, their utter abnegation of the world. An enthusiastic religion had swallowed them up and made them willing to become wanderers and vagabonds on the face of the earth - for his sake to dwell in dens and caves, to be torn asunder, and to be persecuted in every form. Before this degree of devotion Satan saw he had no chance. Such people, as these, he knew, must ultimately subdue the world.

Therefore the arch-enemy said, *'What must I do? I shall lose my supremacy as the god of this world.'* No use to bring in a gigantic system of error which everybody would see to be error. That has never been Satan's way; his plan has been to get hold of a good man here and there who shall creep in, as the apostle said, unawares and preach another doctrine, and who shall deceive, if it were possible, the very elect. And he did it! He accomplished his design. He gradually lowered the standard of Christian life and character, and though, in every revival, God has raised it again to a certain extent, we have never got back thoroughly to the simplicity, purity, and devotion set before us in the Acts of the Apostles.

There it is, a glorious standard put before us. The power is proffered, the conditions are laid down, and we can all attain to it - a real, living, self-sacrificing, hardworking, triumphing religion, and the world will be influenced by it.

Thou hast left thy first love ... repent, and do the first works ... He that hath an ear, let him hear what the Spirit saith unto the churches.
REVELATION 2:4,5,7

THE COMMISSION

I have been reading of late the New Testament with special reference to the aggressive spirit of primitive Christianity, and it is wonderful what floods of light come upon you when you read the Bible with reference to any particular topic on which you are seeking for help. People say they don't see this or that; no, because they do not wish to see. They are not willing to walk in it, and therefore, they do not get it; but those who are willing to obey shall have all the light they want.

It seems to me that we come infinitely short of any right and rational idea of the aggressive spirit of the New Testament saints. Satan has got Christians to accept what I call a namby-pamby, kid-glove kind of system of presenting the gospel to the people. It seems to me this is utterly antagonistic and repugnant to the spirit of the early saints: *'Go ye , and preach the gospel to every creature.'* And again the same idea - *'Unto whom now I send thee.'* Look what is implied in these commissions.

Divesting our minds of all conventionalities and traditionalisms, what would the language mean? *'Go ye!'* To whom? *'To every creature.'* Where am I to get at them? *Where they are. 'Every creature.'* There is the extent of your commission. Seek them out; run after them wherever you can get at them.

Go ye into all the world, and preach the gospel to every creature.
MARK 16:15

DIGNITY

When the Church and the world can jog along comfortably together you may be sure there is something wrong. The world has not altered. Its spirit is exactly the same as it ever was, and if Christians were equally faithful and devoted to the Lord, and separated from the world, living so that their lives were a reproof of all ungodliness, the world would hate them as much as ever it did. It is the Church that has altered, not the world. You say, *'We should be getting into endless turmoil. There would be uproar.'* Yes. And the Acts of the Apostles is full of stories of uproar.

'But ,' you say, *'wouldn't it be inconsistent with the dignity of the gospel?'* That depends upon the standpoint from which you look at it, upon what really constitutes the dignity of the gospel. Is it human dignity or is it divine? It was a very undignified thing, looked at humanly, (for Christ) to die on a cross between two thieves. (So considered), it was the most undignified thing ever done in this world, and yet, looked at on moral and spiritual grounds, it was the grandest spectacle that ever earth or Heaven gazed upon.

That dignity will never suffer even though you should have to be dragged through the streets with a howling mob at your heels, though you should be tied to a stake, as were the martyrs of old, and surrounded by laughing and taunting fiends that will be a dignity which shall be crowned in Heaven with everlasting glory.

Looking unto Jesus the author and finisher of our faith; who for the joy that was set before him endured the cross, despising the shame, and is set down at the right hand of the throne of God.
HEBREWS 12:2

INFLUENCE

While the early Christians were true to the example and teaching of their Master we never find them bemoaning their lack of ability to attract or to convert people. So mighty was their influence, though comparatively few in number, and insignificant in social position, that wherever they went they were said to have *'turned the world upside down'*, and large and flourishing churches sprang up in all directions.

They did not feel the necessity for any half-way meeting place between themselves and the world; they did not lower the tone of the Christian morality in order to meet the corrupt and heathenish notions of those around them; neither did they abjure their spirituality lest it should disgust them. On the contrary, the apostles and early Christians seem to have had the conviction that the more complete their devotion to their Master - the more separate from the world, the more truly spiritual and divine they were - the greater would be their influence for God, and the greater their success in winning men to Christ. Their preaching was *'with demonstration of the Spirit and power'*, consequently multitudes listened, believed, and turned to the Lord.

And my speech and my preaching was not with enticing words of man's wisdom, but in demonstration of the Spirit and of power; that your faith should not stand in the wisdom of men, but in the power of God.
I CORINTHIANS 2:4,5

MOTIVATIONS

It was not until the primitive Christians began to admit worldly principles of action, and to substitute the material for the spiritual, that their influence began to wane, and their testimony to lose its power. It was the gradual substitution of the human for the divine, the material for the spiritual, that overspread Christendom for ages with papal darkness and death.

During the long night of error and suffering, however, God raised up many witnesses to the sufficiency of the Holy Ghost to attract and convert men - many making long pilgrimages and suffering great privations, in order to visit and converse with those endued with this divine gift.

And when at length the light of the Reformation broke over the nations, this one great lesson was again engraven on the hearts of God's chosen instruments: *'It is not by might, nor by power, but by my Spirit, saith the Lord of hosts.'* Thus, after the lapse of ages, we find the gospel, when preached with the old power, the same mighty instrumentality, both for attracting the multitudes and converting the soul.

This is the word of the Lord unto Zerubbabel ... Not by might, nor by power, but by my spirit, saith the Lord of hosts.
ZECHARIAH 4:6

LIFE

From the Reformation down to the present time, we find that wherever the same gospel has been preached with the same accompanying power, the same results have followed, even when the preacher has been trammelled by a false creed, or beset with hosts of opposing influences. Where the Spirit of the Lord is, *there* spiritual miracles are wrought, and wherever miracles are wrought, the people *will* congregate.

You will perceive that we regard this plea - *'that the gospel fails to attract'* - as a suspicious one. We ask those who urge it, to tell us why it fails. We have no hesitation in saying *only* for want of the Holy Ghost. The great disideratum in connection with all our organisations, societies, churches, agencies, and instrumentalities, is *life, life, life*. The people want a *living gospel*, preached by *living, Spirit-baptised souls*. Dare we, in the light of the past, instead of this divine bread, give them the stone of materialism?

If so, we must prepare for the consequences.

For the law of the Spirit of life in Christ Jesus hath made me free from the law of sin and death.
ROMANS 8:2

SIMPLICITY

Christianity is self-propagating and aggressive and in my opinion will never fully triumph till disentangled from the gigantic systems of worldly policy which men have identified it with. The Kingdom of Christ is not of this world and how strikingly was this truth exemplified by the primitive churches. How gloriously successful were they in the propagation of the truth without any of the ponderous machinery of modern times.

The Lord added to the church daily such as should be saved.
ACTS 2:47

MEASURES

I have read that the law of adoption is the only law laid down in the New Testament with respect to modes and measures. I challenge anybody to find me any other. While the gospel message is laid down with unerring exactness, we are left at perfect freedom to adapt our measures and modes of bringing it to bear upon men to the circumstances, times, and conditions in which we live - free as air. *'I became all things to all men.'* The great apostle of the Gentiles who had thrown off the paraphernalia of Judaism years before became as a Jew that he might win the Jews. The great, strong intellect became as a weak man that he might win the weak.

He conformed himself to the conditions and circumstances of his hearers, in all lawful things, that he might win them; he let no mere conventionalities, or ideas of propriety, stand in his way when it was necessary to abandon them. He was brave as a lion, and hailed a crown of martyrdom like a conquering hero, as he was, yet was willing to submit to anything when the requirements of his mission rendered it necessary.

He adapted himself to the circumstances. He was instant in season and out of season. Adapt your measures to your circumstances and to the necessities of the times in which you live.

I am made all things to all men, that I might by all means save some.
I CORINTHIANS 9:22

FREEDOM

We cannot get the order of a single service from the New Testament, nor can we get the form of government of a single church. There is nothing of this stereotyped routinism in the whole of the New Testament. Why? Now there may be some who may have difficulties in this matter. Here is the principle laid down that you are to adapt your measures to the necessities of the people to whom you minister; you are to take the gospel to them in such modes and habitudes of thought and expression and circumstances as will gain for it from them a hearing.

You are to speak with other tongues - go and preach it to them in such a way as they will look at it and listen to it. In that lesson (1 Corinthians 12) we read what a beautiful freedom from all set form and formula there was! What freedom from the gushing freshness, enthusiasm, and love of those new converts! What scope for the different manifestations of the same Spirit. Everything was not cut and dried. Everything was not pre-arranged. It was left to the operation of the Spirit, and the argument that this has been abused is no argument against it, for then you might argue against every privilege.

Here is abundant evidence that these new converts, each one, had opportunity to witness for Jesus, opportunity and scope to give forth the utterance of his soul, and tell other people how he got saved or the experience the Holy Ghost has wrought in him. And look at the result!

Now there are diversities of gifts, but the same Spirit. And there are differences of administrations, but the same Lord. And there are diversities of operations, but it is the same God which worketh all in all.
1 Corinthians 12:4-6

QUALIFICATIONS

I maintain that the only qualification - the only indispensable qualification - for witnessing for Christ is the Holy Ghost. Paul, expressly, over and over again, abjures all merely human equipment. He expressly declares that these things were not the power, where they existed, but that it was the Holy Ghost. Therefore give me man, woman or child, with the Holy Ghost, full of love and zeal for God, and I say it is a great strength and joy to that convert to testify to the Church and to the world.

The Lord is going to evangelise this land by the simple testimony of people saved from sin and the devil, by his power and grace. He is going to do it by witnessing, as he began.

Read your New Testament on this point, and you will be struck with the amazing amount of evidence for this unconventional kind of service. The world wants some more Pentecosts. When shall Peters and Marys be so filled with the Spirit that they cannot help telling what God has done for them, like the woman of Samaria, who, when she had found him of whom Moses and the prophets wrote, went and fetched her fellow-townsmen and women to hear him?

He wishes you to do the same, and this is the way the Lord is going to gather out his great and glorious Kingdom in these latter days - by the power of testimony in the Holy Ghost. He only wants witnesses to be able to go and say, *'We speak that we do know'* - that is the qualification.

No man can say that Jesus is the Lord, but by the Holy Ghost.
1 CORINTHIANS 12:3

REVELATIONS

Jesus Christ, instead of working a miracle, which he never did when it was unnecessary, chose the weak things of the earth to confound the mighty. He would, in the other case, have had first to have untaught all those scribes and doctors almost all they had learned. He would have had to set them free from the bonds of traditionalism. He would have had to remould their minds and then equip them.

There was no necessity for this when he found the fishermen ready to his hand. They were just the men he wanted. They only required tempering with the Holy Ghost and they were ready for the work. The thought as the people thought, they spoke with and associated with the people, and, in fact, were of them. As he wanted the masses of men evangelised, he chose men from amongst the masses to evangelise them.

Here was infinite wisdom: *'I thank thee, O Father, that thou hast hid these things from the wise and prudent, and hast revealed them unto babes. Even so, Father, for so it seemed good in thy sight.'* But he had a purpose in it that the gospel might be propagated in all climes and conditions of men. Any person who has experienced its power in their souls may go and speak it to anybody they can get to hear them and everywhere! We are as free as air and sunlight as to our choice of agencies, and it is time the Church woke up to this.

In that hour Jesus rejoiced in spirit, and said, I thank thee, O Father, Lord of heaven and earth, that thou hast hid these things from the wise and prudent, and hast revealed them unto babes: even so, Father; for so it seemed good in thy sight.
LUKE 10:21

ESSENTIALS

We deem it a great mistake to suppose that any human learning, any human eloquence, any human qualification whatever fits a man or woman for ministering God's Word or dealing with souls.

Whatever else there is or is not, there must be the equipment of the Holy Ghost for, without him, all qualifications, wise as well as foolish, high as well as low, are utterly powerless for the regeneration of mankind.

Howbeit when he, the Spirit of truth, is come, he will guide you into all truth.
JOHN 16:13

WITNESSES

God needs witnesses in this world. Why? Because the whole world is in revolt against him. The world has gone away from God. The world ignores God, denies and contradicts his testimony, misunderstands his character, government, and purposes, and is gone off into utter and universal revolt and rebellion. Now if God is to keep any hold upon man at all, and have any influence with him, he must be represented down here. There was no other way of doing it.

If a province of this realm were in anarchy and rebellion, unless there be some persons in the province whose duty it is to represent the Queen and her Government, it would lapse altogether and be lost to the kingdom for ever. So God must be represented, and, praise his name, he has had his faithful witnesses from the beginning unto now. As the apostle says, *'He left not himself without witness.'*

Down from the days of Enoch who walked with God, to this present hour, God has always had his true and faithful witnesses. In the worst times there have been some burning and shining lights. Sometimes few and far between, sometimes, like Noah, one solitary man in a whole generation of men, witnessing for God - but one, at least, there has been.

God has not left himself without witnesses.

He that speaketh truth sheweth forth righteousness.
PROVERBS 12:17
We ... were eyewitnesses of his majesty.
2 PETER 1:16

MISSION

The Lord commissioned his disciples to be his witnesses, and he said, *'As thou hast sent me into the world, even so I send them into the world.'*

Now, the fact that witnessing is necessary shows that *there is controversy going on in the world* as to the things and claims of God - that there are two sides to this. The great masses of mankind say that God's truth is a lie. They say it virtually, if they do not say it in words, and many thousands of them in words also. They deny, many of them, his very existence and say there is neither Heaven nor Hell; that Jesus Christ was a mere man; that religion is a myth; and that there is no such thing as the knowledge of forgiveness of sins - that this witnessing is a grand delusion of the imagination, and nothing further.

Now, Christ calls his people to go and be witnesses to these facts. Witnesses, you know, must deal with facts, not theories - not what they merely think, or suppose, or have heard, but what they *know*.

As thou hast sent me into the world, even so have I also sent them into the world.
JOHN 17:18
That which we have seen and heard declare we unto you.
1 JOHN 1:3

ILLUMINATION

The faithful witness must give the whole truth; and he must give it personally, too. A faithful witness must give it himself. He can't witness by proxy.

God will say to him: *'If I have put my candle in you, it is that it may shine for somebody else's benefit. If I have given you the bread of life, it is for you to go and break it to the famishing multitudes round about you. Ye are my witnesses.'* You may pay the minister and the missionary, but you must do it yourself, too, for how can *one* witness make up for *two?*

True God wants the minister to witness but that will not make up for your lack of service. *You* must witness; and *there are some souls with whom you have more influence than any other living being* - some souls that you can better get at than any other person; some souls that, if you do not save, will probably never be saved at all.

'Ye are my witnesses, and if ye have the grace and love and light of God, it is at the peril of your soul if you hide it.'

Ye are the light of the world. A city that is set on a hill cannot be hid.
MATTHEW 5:14

SPEAK OUT

Faithful witnesses must speak out, not mince the matter - not *'mumble'*, as they say in court. The judge makes the witness speak up so that everybody may hear him. *He must be heard.* Speak out. And why should not the Lord's witnesses speak out?

David rejoiced to tell of God's righteousness before the great congregation. He was always telling about his goodness, and his law, and singing about it all the day long, dancing before the ark sometimes, and doing all manner of demonstrative things to glorify his God.

And that was not enough, for when he had called upon all humankind to praise him, he called on the hills and the trees to clap their hands and dance for joy. We want some of *that* sort of religion nowadays. Talk of the new dispensation, I wish we could get a bit of the old one back!

Let the redeemed of the Lord say so, whom he hath redeemed from the hand of the enemy.
PSALM 107:2

OUTSPOKENNESS

The interests of truth demand outspokenness. How is error to be met but by the bold proclamation of the truth? How are the emissaries of Satan palming upon mankind his lies - always at it, night and day - how are they silenced but by witnesses faithfully crying in their ears, *'This is a lie and that is a lie. This is the truth and this is the way; we know, we see, we feel - walk ye in it.'*

They want outspoken witnesses now, as there ever were, and what does Jesus Christ want? He wants his true witnesses to come out and face them, and be a match for them - not to sneak away in holes and corners and be ashamed of their religion, and talk about an unobtrusive religion - unobtrusive nonsense! There is no such thing.

Come out before the world.

Now when they saw the boldness of Peter and John ...
they took knowledge of them, that they had been with
Jesus.
ACTS 4:13

How do you read your Bibles? How do you read the history of the miracles - the stories of his opening the eyes, unstopping the ears, cleansing the leper, and raising the dead? The Lord show us how to read it. He will heal you if you will let him. These are the sort of words the world wants - the living words, living embodiments of Christianity, walking embodiments of the Spirit, and life and power of Jesus Christ.

You may scatter Bibles, as you have done, all over the world. You may preach, and sing, and talk, and do what you will; but if you don't exhibit to the people *living epistles,* show them the transformation of character and life in yourself which is brought about by the power and grace of God - if you don't go to them and do the works of Jesus Christ, you may go on preaching, and the world will get worse and worse, and the Church too.

We want a living embodiment of Christianity. We want *Jesus to come in the flesh again.*

Ye are our epistle written in our hearts, known and read of all men: Forasmuch as ye are manifestly declared to be the epistle of Christ ministered by us, written not with ink, but with the Spirit of the living God; not in tables of stone, but in fleshy tables of the heart.
2 CORINTHIANS 3:2,3.

GLORY

When they had prayed, the place was shaken. What was involved in that prayer - what does it mean? Why did the glory come? Why did the Holy Ghost overshadow them? Why wer they filled with God - so filled that they had to go down and could not help themselves, but went into the streets and poured it out upon the godless multitudes around them? Why, why did it come? Why do hundreds of assemblies of God's people meet and pray, but nothing comes? They hold long meetings and make long prayers, and sing, *'We are waiting for the fire,'* but nothing comes. Why did it come on that particular occasion? Because in that prayer was thorough, entire, everlasting self-abandonment. They came up caring for nothing but pleasing God and doing as he bade them - and the Holy Ghost alone knows when a soul arrives at that point. He will never come till the soul *does* arrive at that point.

And when they had prayed, the place was shaken where they were assembled together; and they were all filled with the Holy Ghost, and they spake the word of God with boldness.
ACTS 4:31

PROMISES

God's promises are made to righteous people ... who are, firstly, in fellowship with him. Having been brought into living fellowship by a living faith, the promises are made to those people who *maintain* that union and who avail themselves of the opportunities and privileges which Jesus has bestowed upon them by virtue of that union.

Now, you see, it is not enough that you were *once* in union with Jesus, in order to get answers to your prayers. don't you see, the first condition is wanting? There is no possible way of approach to the Father but through the Son. And that does not mean saying, *'For the sake of the Lord Jesus Christ.'* It does not matter much what people *say*, it is what they *mean* and feel he pays attention to, and he knows when people really offer their prayers in union with his Son.

Never drop out of living union with Jesus. Keep in it - hold it fast - walk in it, and you will get answers to your prayers every day. You will be as sure of it as if you saw God doing what you ask, and heard him speaking to you. You will be able to say, *'I know that thou hearest me always.'* Bless his name!

If ye abide in me, and my words abide in you, ye shall ask what ye will, and it shall be done unto you.
JOHN 15:7

CONFIDENCE

What does it mean to walk in the light? Obey his voice. Don't stop to confer with flesh and blood, but, as Paul did, get up and set off to commence the career which your Master commands. That is walking in the light - obeying - not standing quibbling with the Lord about it, but *doing* it.

Did any man that ever got the pearl of great price feel he had given too much for it, even if he had given all that he had? *Never!* Martyrs and confessors have gloried in the possession of it while they have writhed on the rack and in the flames, and you never heard one solitary testimony that any man or woman of God ever thought that they had paid too highly for it. Never!

Do you want to have your prayers answered? That is the way. Walk so that your own heart condemns you not. The obedient child that lives in complacent affection with its parents has no fear in coming to ask for favours. It knows it will get them. Its own heart does not condemn it. I defy any man to separate confidence from obedience. If you will not be obedient you cannot have confidence. I challenge any Christian to tell me that he can go up to the throne of God in faith for any blessing when his own heart condemns him. He knows he cannot. *He has first to get that state of condemnation taken away* before he can exercise faith for any blessing.

Walk in the light, as he is in the light.
I JOHN 1:7
Beloved, if our heart condemn us not, then have we confidence toward God. And whatsoever we ask, we receive of him, because we keep his commandments, and do those things that are pleasing in his sight.
1 JOHN 3:21,22

EXERCISING FAITH

No believer can exercise faith for anything that the Holy Ghost does not lead him up to. You may pray, and pray, but you will never exercise faith until you have the spirit making intercession in you. There is very little difficulty about believing with people who have taken the three preceding steps. Those who are in fellowship with Jesus, those who are walking in the light, those who have the Holy Ghost as an interceding Spirit - they know what to pray for; they know what the mind of the Spirit is; they know how the Spirit is leading them, and they can march up to the throne and *'ask and receive'*. They know their request is according to the mind of God, and they can wrestle, if need be, like the Syrophenician woman, if he sees fit to try their faith. He does not always answer at once. he lets them wrestle with groans that cannot be uttered; but they know they will get it, because they know the Spirit is making intercession for them, and they hold on sometimes amidst great discouragement and temptation, till the answer comes. They get the assurance of faith which says, *'Yes, it shall be done.'* People look at them in wonder. Christian friends know the thing they are praying for has not come, and say, *'You look as glad as if you had it.'* I know it is coming; I have the assurance that it shall be done.

If any of you lack wisdom, let him ask of God, that giveth to all men liberally, and upbraideth not; and it shall be given him. But let him ask in faith, nothing wavering.
JAMES 1:5,6

AGONY OF SOUL

Prayer is agony of soul - wrestling of the Spirit. You know how man and women deal with another when they are in desperate earnestness of something to be done. That is prayer, ..., and when you get your heart influenced, and melted, and wrought up, and burdened by the Holy Ghost for souls, you will never pray but somebody will be convinced - some poor soul's dark blind eyes will be opened, and spiritual life commence.

Likewise the Spirit also helpeth our infirmities: for we know not what we should pray for as we ought; but the Spirit itself maketh intercession for us with groanings which cannot be uttered.
ROMANS 8:26

SEND IT

Some speak of the work of salvation as God's work. Yes, truly, but he gives *'the treasure in earthen vessels'*. What did he tell Paul? *'I will send thee!'* What for? Listen to God's order: *'to open their eyes'*. Yes, that comes first. *'To turn them from darkness to light.'* What, *Paul* do that? Yes, and what next? *'From the power of Satan unto God.'*

There you have it - it is God's work through us. Some say, *'Do it quietly, reality is sober.'* Well now, Jude says people are saved, *saved* under various outward conditions. *'Save them with fear, pulling them out of the pit,'* and *we will, we do,* by the hair of the head almost, if necessary!

At a prayer meeting of which I read some years ago, an old man was asking for a blessing and for salvation for some whom he knew. *'Let it come,'* he said, *'like the gentle dew upon the mown grass, like the small rain upon the tender herb.'* Presently, a young brother, when he had borne it as long as he could, stood up: *'Oh, Lord!'* he cried, *'don't take any notice, we will only ask thee that it may come. We want thy salvation, we don't care how it comes, we will not dictate to thee, only send it, send it anyhow! Amen!'*

Thy name shall be no more Jacob, but Israel: for as a prince hast thou power with God and with men, and hast prevailed.
GENESIS 32:28

MYSTERY

The mystery of godliness is great, but it is given to the real followers of Jesus *'to know the mysteries of the Kingdom'*, as far as is needful for them. But Satan makes so much ado about the mysteries of grace, as though mystery were peculiar to *it*, when all nature is enveloped in mystery and what can be more mysterious than *thought?* What is thought, memory, emotion? How does thought arise? How does memory store up and hide and years after pour forth its awful or pleasing treasure? Who can explain these common operations of the mind? And what in the Bible is more mysterious? And yet I am conscious that I *think* and remember as that I live and breathe.

All is mystery around me, above me, below me, within me, before me, but yet I believe, act, plan, live, according to what I *can* understand, and must be content to await the solutions of these mysteries at some future enlargement and enlightenment of my faculties.

Without controversy great is the mystery of godliness.
1 TIMOTHY 3:16

LIKE JESUS

I think it must be self-evident that it is *the most important question* that can possibly occupy the mind of men - *how much like God can we be,* how near to God we can come on earth preparatory to our being perfectly like him, and living, as it were, in his very heart for ever and ever in Heaven. Anyone who has any measure of the Spirit of God must perceive that this is the most important question on which we can concentrate our thoughts; and the mystery of mysteries to me is how anyone with any measure of the Spirit of God can help looking at this blessing of holiness, and saying, *'Well, even if it does seem too great for attainment on earth it is very beautiful and very blessed. I wish I could attain it.' That,* it seems to me, must be the attitude of every person who has the Spirit of God - that he should hunger and thirst after it, and feel that he shall never be satisfied till he wakes up in the lovely likeness of his Saviour.

Beloved, now are we the sons of God, and it doth not yet appear what we shall be: but we know that, when he shall appear, we shall be like him; for we shall see him as he is.
1 JOHN 3:2

RESTORATION

We are told over and over again that God wants his people to be pure and that *purity in their hearts is the very central idea and end and purpose of the gospel of Jesus Christ.*

God wants us just *to be* and *to do*. He wants us to be like his Son and then to do as his Son did, and when we come to that he will shake the world through us. People say, *'You can't be like his Son.'* Very well, then, you will never get any more than you believe for. If I did not think Jesus Christ *strong* enough to destroy the works of the devil and bring us back to God's original pattern, I would throw the whole thing up for ever. What! He has given us a religion we cannot practice? I say, no, he has not come to mock us. What! He has given us a Saviour who cannot save? Then I decline to have anything to do with him. What! Does he profess to do for me what he cannot? No, no, no. He *'is not a man, that he should lie; neither the Son of man, that he should repent.'*

I tell you that his scheme of salvation is two-sided - it is Godward and manward. It contemplates me as well as it contemplates the great God. It is not a scheme of salvation merely - it is a scheme of *restoration.*

Likewise reckon ye also yourselves to be dead indeed unto sin, but alive unto God through Jesus Christ our Lord. Let not sin therefore reign in your mortal body, that ye should obey it in the lusts thereof ... but yield your-selves unto God, as those that are alive from the dead ...
ROMANS 6:11-13

SINCERITY

What is the meaning of the term, *'perfect heart'*, referring to the hearts of God's children all the way through the Bible? As you know, I like to establish my points in the mouths of two or three witnesses. Look at Psalm 37:37 - *'Mark the perfect man, and behold the upright: for the end of that man is peace.' ...'Be ye perfect,'* says the Saviour, *'even as your Father which is in heaven is perfect.'* And again, *'Howbeit we speak wisdom among them that are perfect.'* 1 Corinthians 2:6.

There are a number of others, but these are samples, signifying a great difference between the persons who are spoken of and ordinary men and women. Now, what do we mean? Well, the very lowest rendering of all divines and all schools is this, that it means *sincerity* and *thoroughness*. Well, that is all I want. Give me a man sincere and thorough in his love and that is all I want; that will stretch through all the ramifications of his existence. That is what I mean by holiness! It means that a man is wholehearted in love and thoroughly out-and-out in service.

For the eyes of the Lord run to and fro throughout the whole earth, to shew himself strong in the behalf of them whose heart is perfect toward him.
2 Chronicles 16:9

DAVID'S EXAMPLE

What is a perfect heart? Firstly, a heart perfect in its loyalty to God, thoroughly given over to God's side, irrespective of consequences, *loyal*. These are the hearts that God wants. This was the difference between David and Saul. There was not so much difference in the greater part of Saul's outward life, when compared with David. The difference was that David was loyal to God, and for that reason, God calls him a man after his own heart.

From the first calling of David from the sheepfolds, right to the end, with one or two exceptions, during the whole of his life he was loyal to God. The interests of God's Kingdom lay at David's heart - not his own honour, ease, or aggrandisement; not his own fame or riches, or building himself a house - it was the house of God that was dear to his heart.

He was loyal, whereas Saul was loyal only as far as it served his own purposes and interests. When God's commandments went counter to his notions, he openly set God at naught and did as he liked. He sacrificed God's interests to his own. He was unloyal at heart, hence he was a traitor, and never could learn the way of the Lord. He was never perfect towards the Lord his God, and, at last, God cast him off. Just the difference between the two - loyal and unloyal.

Mark the perfect man, and behold the upright: for the end of that man is peace.
PSALM 37:37

DANIEL'S EXAMPLE

A heart perfect towards God means perfect in its *obedience*. That man or woman who has this kind of heart ceases to pick and choose amongst the commandments of God which he shall obey and which not.

The moment you show yourself thorough, that moment will he show himself strong for you.

Daniel was one of the perfect-hearted men; he served his God when he was in prosperity. He set his window open every day. Then his enemies got round the king to make a decree that no man should pray but to this king for so many days. *'Now,'* they said, *'we shall have him.'* But Daniel just did as he was wont, he went and prayed with his window open.

You say that was demonstrative religion, that was courting opposition. What need was there for him to make this display; could he not have shut the window and go into an inner room? Because he would be thorough for his God in adversity, in the face of enemies, as he was in prosperity. So he went and prayed with open window to the God of heaven, and because *he is* the God of Heaven, he is able to take care of his own.

His heart was perfect towards the Lord his God.

Mine eyes shall be upon the faithful of the land, that they may dwell with me; he that walketh in a perfect way, he shall serve me.
PSALM 101:6

ABRAHAM'S EXAMPLE

A perfect heart is perfect in its trust. Perhaps that ought to come first, for it is the very root of all.

How beautiful Abraham was in the eyes of God. How do we know that Abraham had a perfect heart towards God? Because he trusted him. No other proof - no less proof - would have been of any use. I dare say he was compassed with infirmities, had many erroneous views, manward and earthward, but his heart was perfect towards God. Do you think God would have failed in his promise to Abraham?

Abraham trusted him almost to the blood of Isaac, and God showed himself strong on his behalf, and delivered him, and made him the father of the faithful; crowned him with everlasting honour, so that his name, from generation to generation, has been a pillar of strength to the Lord's people, and a crown of glory to his God.

The Lord appeared to Abram, and said unto him, I am the Almighty God; walk before me, and be thou perfect.
GENESIS 17:1

GRACE AND POWER

I want to define the blessing of sanctification as we believe it and as I believe God will show it to those who really and honestly want to understand or rather experience it, because it is one of those mysteries of divine love and grace that you will never understand until you experience. Then I want to guard my definition by noting some things which are often mistaken for it.

It is not freedom from infirmity either in mind or body. It is not necessary for the accomplishment of his redeeming purpose that we should be made perfect again, in the way of apprehension, memory or capacity. This was not necessary for our redemption, or he would have provided it; but he left us still physically imperfect. He can save us from sin in our present crippled state of body and of mind, and it magnifies his grace the more.

When we speak of sanctification or holiness, we do not mean a man is saved from simple infirmity. He *is* saved from allowing his infirmities to degenerate into sin or leading him into sin. He is enabled to make the same use of his infirmities as Paul did who said, *'I glory in mine infirmities also that the power of Christ may rest upon me.'* That is, through my weak body and imperfect mind I may the more magnify the grace and power of his salvation.

Most gladly therefore will I rather glory in my infirmities, that the power of Christ may rest upon me.
2 CORINTHIANS 12:9

TEMPTATION

Sanctification does not mean deliverance from temptation. There are some sincere souls who I think are in bondage on this point. I tried to illustrate this on a previous occasion by showing how Christ transcended the law, when I went rather fully into the temptation of the Saviour, showing that was not sin, and that *while you stand firm* and resist, the greater the temptation, the greater the sympathy Christ has with you, *'for he was tempted in all points.'* I will never let that go. *'Like as we are, yet without sin.'*

There are no difficulties which apply to this point to the sanctified soul which did not apply to Jesus Christ. A man's sensibilities can be excited to the highest degree: he can be as hungry as Jesus was when he came out of that forty days fast, when no doubt his whole being was prostrate, for he was perfect man as well as perfect God. The devil took that occasion to present an unlawful means of satisfying his hunger. *'Resist the devil and he will flee from you.'*

Saying yes to temptation is sin - not temptation itself.

There is no necessity to sin you may be severely tempted and yet not sin.

There hath no temptation taken you but such as is common to man: but God is faithful, who will not suffer you to be tempted above that ye are able; but will with the temptation also make a way to escape, that ye may be able to bear it.
1 CORINTHIANS 10:13

MATURITY

Sanctification is not final growth. It does not imply final attainment. You must discriminate between purity and maturity. You may have the perfect baby but he is not a man yet. He has to grow and develop and increase; but people really and truly do not begin to grow in grace until they are sanctified. It is more frequently a falling down and a getting up again than an even onward progress in grace and salvation. Hence if you really want to grow in grace, if you want to rise to the possibilities of your nature in the salvation of God, you must be delivered from sin, for sin undoes you, knocks you down in the mud, as it were, and you have to be, as the apostle says, *always laying the foundation for repentance from dead works.'*

How can such people grow?

Let us go on unto perfection ...
HEBREWS 6:1
But grow in grace, and in the knowledge of our Lord and Saviour Jesus Christ.
2 PETER 3:18

TRANSFORMATION

We believe sanctification, to be deliverance from sin - full conformity of heart, and mind, and will, to the law and mind of God. It is having the heart circumcised to keep his law, having his Spirit in us causing us to walk in all his statutes and ordinances blamelessly, an inward transformation into the very likeness of Christ, a purifying of the motives, purposes, desires, affections of the soul, and a thorough committal on the side of God and right at all costs.

That is what we understand by holiness and will anybody dare to say this is more than God calls us to? As Doddridge said, *'If you are not aiming after the highest attainments in Christ, you are not in a state of grace at all.'* The very least measure of the Spirit of God sets a soul longing after the fulness.

He can no more rest without it than the angels of Heaven could. he is hungering and thirsting from the time he gets saved until he is filled and satisfied with the righteousness which Jesus Christ promised.

The blood of Jesus Christ his Son cleanseth us from all sin.
1 JOHN 1:7

HOLINESS

I argue that holiness is attainable *because it is expressly, emphatically and repeatedly commanded.* Jesus Christ, whose teachings were all, or nearly all, prospective, concludes one of his addresses with saying, *'Be ye therefore perfect, even as your Father which is in Heaven is perfect.'* What does he mean? It must at least mean that in our measure and according to our capacity we are perfectly to fulfil the law of benevolence as God does with his capacity.

Then again the first great commandment was never abrogated and never will be. *'Thou shalt love the Lord thy God with all thy heart, and with all thy soul, and with all thy mind, and with all thy strength.'* And the second is like unto it, *'Thy neighbour as thyself.'*

This first and greatest commandment remains in force today as much as it ever was, and must continue in force throughout eternity. It must ever remain the duty of the creature to love his fellow as himself. Must it not?

Now, as God never requires anything which he does not give us power to perform, he has included this experience in the provisions of grace.

But as he which hath called you is holy, so be ye holy in all manner of conversation; Because it is written, Be ye holy; for I am holy.
1 Peter 1:15,16

LOST INTEGRITY

I argue the attainability of holiness, from the provisions of the gospel. *Christ has undertaken this work. What has he undertaken?*

You say he has undertaken the mediatorial work to bring us back to God. Yes, but the mediatorial work was two-fold: it was Godward and it was manward. Christ, as it were, put one hand on the justice of God and the other on the sinfulness of man, and he undertook to satisfy the one by removing the other. He made atonement - a perfect, everlasting sacrifice for our sins, but it was restorative as well as atoning. The manward aspect of the atonement was to bring us back to complete and eternal harmony with God. He came to restore as well as atone; to bring us back to our lost integrity and purity, and this was what made the atonement necessary. Hence, *'the Son of man was manifested that he might destroy the works of the devil.'*

Where? In the heart of man. What constitutes the essence of sin? Rebellion. Now what is necessary in the nature of the case for God to win completely back again such a rebel at heart? It is of no use subduing me merely; he must renew me.

This is the end of the commandment, *'Love out of a pure heart.'* This is the centre of the scheme of redemption. If God could have saved you short of that he could have saved you without Christ at all but he must have you back *cured of your sin*, pure in heart.

Now the God of peace, that brought again from the dead our Lord Jesus, that great shepherd of the sheep, through the blood of the everlasting covenant, make you perfect in every good work to do his will, working in you that which is well pleasing in his sight, through Jesus Christ.
HEBREWS 13:20-21

I argue the attainability of holiness because it is repeatedly made the object of inspired prayer.

Jesus prayed for his disciples, *'Sanctify them through thy truth,'* and also, *'As thou, Father, art in me and I in thee, that they also may be one in us.'* Paul prays for the Thessalonians, *'And the very God of peace sanctify you wholly and I pray God your whole spirit and soul and body be preserved blameless unto the coming of our Lord Jesus Christ.'*

There are many other texts of similar import, but these are sufficient, for surely neither Christ nor Paul could possibly have prayed for an experience in believers which they knew to be impossible. Such prayers would be utterly incompatible with manly sincerity, much less with godly sincerity. All that is needed for us to experience an answer to these and such like prayers is that we second them by an earnest and determined desire to have them fulfilled in our experience.

Do you go with what I have state thus far? If so, I want to make it plain to you that the Lord is calling you to this experience, not setting you a task which you are unable to perform. Some people say we are to aim at the standard of holiness, but that we must not expect ever to attain it. This seems to me trifling with the most solemn of obligations and judging God to be less wise and reasonable than man.

And the very God of peace sanctify you wholly; and I pray God your whole spirit and soul and body be preserved blamelss unto the coming of our Lord Jesus Christ.
1 THESSALONIANS 5:23

WASHED IN THE BLOOD

If there is needed any further proof of the attainability of this experience of holiness, it seems to me a most convincing proof that, in almost every instance where our reception into Heaven is referred to, there is the recognition of antecedent purity of character. Search out these references for yourselves, but let us take two or three as specimens. *'Blessed are the dead which die in the Lord they may rest from their labours; and their works do follow them.'* Their works, that is, their antecedent character, follow them. *'Blessed are they that do his commandments, that they may enter in through the gates into the city.'* They that do his will, which must mean being holy.

Again, speaking of the Lamb's wife: *'To her was granted that she should be arrayed in fine linen, clean and white, [which is] the righteousness of the saints.'* Again, referring to the multitudes arrayed in white, the angel said, *'These are they which came out of great tribulation, and have washed their robes and made them white in the blood of the Lamb.'* Washed them, of course, while here on earth and made them white which signifies holiness.

Follow peace with all men, and holiness, without which no man shall see the Lord.
HEBREWS 12:14

BE DEFINITE

Indefiniteness in spiritual things is of the devil. You don't like indefiniteness in your temporal affairs. You know it betrays something wrong. When a man comes to you with a great deal of palaver, and makes a sort of general proclamation of his good intentions towards you, and yet refuses to come to any definite point, you feel that his protestations don't count for much.

Now, I ask, is it possible that the great God has dealt with me indefinitely in that which most concerns my eternal destiny? Impossible!

Then be definite with God. Know what you want and seek *that*. Separate this blessing from all its accidental surroundings. Don't confound it with abounding joy. This sometimes accompanies it, and sometimes not. Don't confound it with any particular means or modes, for the ways by which God brings souls into this experience are quite as diversified as the ways by which he brings them into pardon and peace at first.

Realise what it is you want. Salvation from that which has been your bane, your torment, from that which has tripped you up many a time and sent you on your face before God with bitter crying and tears - salvation *from sin*. Go to God, wait on him, and comply with the conditions he has laid down and *you will get* what you seek.

But now being made free from sin, and become servants to God, ye have your fruit unto holiness and the end everlasting life.
ROMANS 6:22

123

SUNLIGHT

You must allow the Spirit to work in you a godly sorrow for all sins of backsliding and unfaithfulness of the past. I fear many Christians fly off here, as soon as the Spirit begins to deal with them by revealing the hidden depths of their hearts, they give up. As one said, *'I feel as if I had never been converted at all. He has opened up such depths of depravity in my heart, I seem worse than ever.'* I said that is just what God does for all souls previous to cleansing. He shows you the depth of the disease that you may take hold of the Physician with that degree of faith which is necessary for perfect cleansing.

He will show it all to you, and make you loathe yourself in dust and ashes. In fact the conviction and sorrow that a soul often goes through in this state is far greater than at conversion, because its perceptions are so deepened that God is better able to deal with it, and if you will only abide the process he will make a perfect cure and put a song of thanksgiving in your mouth and give you the sunlight of his smile continually.

Search me, O God, and know my heart: try me, and know my thoughts: and see if there be any wicked way in me, and lead me in the way everlasting.
PSALM 139:23,24.

CONSECRATION

There are *two indispensable conditions of attaining God's blessing - entire consecration and faith in his promises.*

Consecration is generally the defective point. When people come to this, they have but little trouble about faith, but, oh, the subtlety of the human heart, how it will go round one particular spot. How it will argue: *'Well, but this is such a little thing. God can't require this.'* (But) *while you have respect for consequences your consecration is not entire.*

You see what consecration means. It means I don't care what happens. I will have this salvation if it is to be had. When you come to that you will get it; that is the point. If I were asked where I believe thousands of believers stand today, I would say, just there. They are standing where Abraham stood when the Lord called him from his father's house and his native land into a land which he knew not and which he was only *afterwards* to receive for an inheritance.

They are standing there, but they are not doing as Abraham did - coming out and obeying - they are standing there arguing, hesitating and halting. And there they have been for years. You will have to get over that bar and say, *'Here goes, Lord, if I lose all I'm going all lengths with thee.'*

That is consecration.

By faith Abraham, when he was called to go out into a place which he should after receive for an inheritance, obeyed; and he went out, not knowing whither he went.
HEBREWS 11:8

The second condition is faith. When you have come thus far then you must believe - trust. I have talked with hundreds and as a rule they have not found much difficulty about faith when consecration has been thorough. Still, there are exceptions, because there are two mistakes made on this point. There are some anxious souls whom Satan gets to be always consecrating, but never trusting.

The other mistake is that people try to trust but don't truly consecrate, and so they get no further.

Now, what God hath joined together let us not be so foolish as to put asunder. We are to consecrate - that is our part. We are to be thorough and sincere and allow the Holy Spirit to have his way. Let us be sincere, but when we *have* the testimony of his Spirit that he has searched and revealed us, and that we do thus consecrate ourselves then let us *claim the blessing*. Let us believe then that having cleansed the temple he now comes in and *takes possession*. Sanctification does not mean that Christ comes and works in me and then departs to Heaven to look on and see if I maintain it. No, he truly does a divine work in me, but he cleanses the temple *for himself*, for his own use.

And is he not able to keep that clean which he has cleansed? If he could do the greater work is he not able to do the lesser? Yes, he can, and all you have to do is to let him do so, walking by faith in humble submissive obedience to the light he gives.

Them which are sanctified by faith that is in me.
ACTS 26:18

126

STRENGTH

Satan tempts you to shrink from a full consecration for fear you should not be able to live up to it; but if you will comply with the conditions, God will fulfil this promise. If you will only yield yourself up without reserve, he will work in you to will and to do of his good pleasure. Hear your Lord's word: *'If a man love me, he will keep my words: and my Father will love him, and we will come unto him, and make our abode with him.'* Surely, with the Father and the Son, you will be able to do and suffer all things. The reason for your past failures has been the *want* of God. When God comes to dwell in you, his strength will be made perfect in your weakness; you will be able to do all things through Christ.

I doubt not some of you are saying, *'How shall I realise the fulfilment of these blessed promises?'* I answer, by simple faith. Just as you trusted at first for justification, and rested not on your feelings but on his promises, so now you must cast yourself on his blessed assurances of healing and of strength.

My grace is sufficient for thee: for my strength is made perfect in weakness.
2 CORINTHIANS 12:9

BEGIN AT ONCE

There are certain laws which govern success in the kingdom of grace as well as in the kingdom of nature, and you must study these laws and adapt yourself to them. It would be in vain for the husbandman to scatter his seed over the unbroken ground or on pre-occupied soil. You must plough and harrow and put your seed in carefully, and in proper proportion, and at the right time, and then you must water and weed and wait for the harvest.

And just so in divine things. The laws of the spiritual kingdom are quite as certain and unerring in their operation as the laws of the natural kingdom, and, perhaps, a great deal more so. But through the blindness and obtuseness and unbelief of our hearts we could not, or would not, find them out.

People get up and fluster about and expect to be able to work for God without any thought or care or trouble. For the learning of earthly professions they will give years of labour and thought, but in work for God they do not seem to think it worthwhile to take trouble to think and ponder, to plan and experiment, to try means, to pray and wrestle with God for wisdom. Then they fail, grow discouraged, and give up.

This is not the way to begin to work for God. Begin as soon as you like, begin at once, but begin in the right way. Begin by praying him to show you how, and to equip you for the work, and begin in a humble, submissive, teachable spirit.

Another parable put he forth unto them, saying, The kingdom of Heaven is likened unto a man which sowed good seed in his field.
MATTHEW 13:24

STUDY YOUR PLANS

Study the New Testament with special reference to working for God and you will be surprised how every page of it will give you increased light. You will see that God holds you absolutely responsible for every iota of capacity and influence he has given you, that he expects you to improve every moment of your time, every faculty of your being, every particle of your influence, and every penny of your money *for him*. When once you get *this* light, it will be a marvellous guide in all the other particulars and ramifications of your life. Men in earthly warfare study plans of stratagem, and adopt measures in order that they may take the enemy by surprise! But how little care and attention God's people give to taking souls; and yet it is *far harder work to take souls than it is to take cities*.

I say those who want to be successful in winning souls require to watch not only days but nights. They (need) much of the Holy Ghost, for it is true still *'this kind can come forth by nothing, but by prayer and fasting'*. We have grown wiser than our Lord nowadays; but, I tell you, it is the same old-fashioned way, and if you want to pour out living waters upon souls you will have to drink largely at the fountain yourself. May God rouse us up.

This kind can come forth by nothing, but by prayer and fasting.
MARK 9:29

DRIVE IT HOME

A qualification for successful labour is power to get the truth home to the heart.

Not to deliver it! I wish the word had never been coined in connection with Christian work. Deliver it, indeed - *that* is not in the Bible! No, no, not deliver it, but *drive it home* - send it in - make it *felt*. That is your work, not merely to say it, not quietly and gently to put it before the people. Here is just the difference between a self-consuming, soul-burdened, Holy Ghost successful ministry, and a careless, happy-go-lucky, easy sort of thing that just rolls it out like a lesson, and goes home holding itself in no way responsible for the consequences.

Here is *all* the difference either in public or individual labour. God has made your responsible, not for delivering the truth, but for getting it home, fixing it in the conscience as a red-hot iron, as a bolt, straight from his throne; and he has placed at your disposal the *power to do it*.

For though I preach the gospel, I have nothing to glory of: for necessity is laid upon me; yea, woe is unto me, if I preach not the gospel!
I Corinthians 9:16

ZEAL

You will never make any other soul realise the verities of eternal things any further than you realise them yourself. You will beget in the soul of your hearer exactly the degree of realisation which the Spirit of God gives to you, and no more; therefore, if you are in a dreamy, cosy, half-asleep condition, you will only beget the same kind of realisation in the souls who hear you. You must be wide awake, quick, alive, feeling deeply in sympathy with the truth you utter, or it will produce no result.

Lord give us a real, robust, living, hardy Christianity, full of zeal and faith, which shall bring into the Kingdom of God lively, well-developed children, full of life and energy. Friends, we want this vivid realisation ourselves. Oh! get hold of God. Ask him to baptize you with his Spirit until the zeal of his house eats you up. This Spirit will burn his way through all obstacles of flesh and blood, of forms, proprieties, and respectabilities. He will burn his way through and produce living and telling results in the hearts of those to whom you speak. Earnestness - such earnestness that it comes to desperation - like that of Paul, who counted all things but dross; yea, and who counted not his life too dear unto him: that is the secret.

His word was in mine heart as a burning fire shut up in my bones, and I was weary with forbearing, and I could not stay.
JEREMIAH 20:9

MONEY

I once heard an old veteran saint say, and I thought it was extravagant at the time: *'I consider the use of money the surest test of a man's character.'* I thought, no, surely his use of his wife and children is a surer test than that, but I have lived to believe his sentiment.

We know it is so by experience and the history of God's people. You must give up your money as an end: it must be all given to God, to whom it belongs, being entirely used for his service. If you want to be a successful labourer for souls, you will have to do that at the threshhold. Give up your money to the Lord. If you think it right to keep some of it, keep it to use it for him as you do, and be strict with yourself and then you will be all right.

It is a narrow and difficult path. I tremble for you who have got it, and I am glad I have not. But as you have got it, I will give you the best advice I know. It is an awful (awesome) thing to have it, but the next best thing is to consecrate it and use it to his glory; and if you do not, it will eat into your soul as doth a canker. To your spiritual nature it will be as a cancer is to your physical nature.

Bring ye all the tithes into the storehouse, that there may be meat in mine house, and prove me now herewith, saith the Lord of hosts, if I will not open you the windows of heaven, and pour you out a blessing, that there shall not be room enough to receive it.
MALACHI 3:10

DUTY

We should never, on any account, allow ourselves to excuse any neglect of God and duty because such neglect is all but universal; we should look at things as they are in the light of the judgment throne; and when we see conduct worthy of condemnation, condemn it, and be determined to separate ourselves in heart and life from evil practices, however much respected they may be, and take our stand on the side of duty and of God at all costs.

How often do I hear the remark, *'We know things are not what they should be'*, from people who have not the slightest intention of striving in any way to make things better, and who would not, on any account incur the odium of expressing any condemnation on that neglect of religious duty which they profess so much to deplore.

Away with this unmanly, unwomanly cowardice! We have the light; let us come to it in order to see whether our deeds, and the deeds of those around us who profess to be working for God, are wrought in him. We can, by God's grace, do our duty, if we will. Christ came on purpose to empower us to do it.

For we must all appear before the judgment seat of Christ; that everyone may receive the things done in his body, according to that he hath done, whether it be good or bad.
2 CORINTHIANS 5:10

STEWARDSHIP

The very idea of service means the remuneration of the will of the servant for the will of the master; the giving up of the personal freedom of the servant to the master; the consecrating of the servant's time and energy and interests to the promotion, not of his own, but the master's interests.

Look at the servants of the Lord Jesus Christ. Is this the idea of the service which God Almighty demands from his servants? Can it be imagined that he requires less than a man requires from his fellows? Is this service less comprehensive? Does it embrace less abandonment of self and less consecration to the interests of God?

If there was one truth that Jesus Christ laboured more persistently to inculcate into the minds of his disciples more than another it was this - that they were not, in any sense, their own; that they absolutely belonged to him, body, soul and spirit. If they were stewards they were to hold their stewardship for him; if they were husbandmen they were to cultivate their ground for him. If they possessed talents they were to improve their talents for him. If they possessed money they were to use it for his interests and not their own. This is assumed in every single parable and is implied in every bit of his teaching.

Moreover it is required in stewards, that a man be found faithful.
1 CORINTHIANS 4:2

PROXY

If religion consists in doing the will of God, what an anomaly is an inactive Christian! Yet there are multitudes in this our day professing to be Christians, who do absolutely nothing for the salvation of souls, or the glory of God. Men and women attempt to serve God by proxy, as though paying another for the employment of his talent were all the same as improving their own; as though God did not demand, and the world need, the exertion of every man's energies and the exhibition of every light which God has kindled.

The babe in Christ must be made to feel his individual untransferable responsibility. He must be taught that labour is the law of life, spiritual as well as natural, and that to increase in wisdom and stature and in favour with God, he *'must be about his Father's business'*.

The capacity of every young convert should be ascertained and a suitable sphere provided for its development.

For we are his workmanship, created in Christ Jesus unto good works, which God hath before ordained that we should walk in them.
EPHESIANS 2:10

135

GOD'S PLAN

I have no hope that God will ever assure us that we shall lose nothing in seeking to do his will. I don't think this is God's plan. I think he sets before us our duty, and then demands its performance, expecting us to leave the consequences with him.

If he had promised *beforehand* to give Abraham his Isaac back again, where would have been that illustrious display of faith and love which has served to encourage and cheer God's people in all ages? If we could always *see* our way, we should not have to wak by faith, but by sight. I know God's professing people are generally as anxious to see their way as worldlings are, but they thus dishonour God and greatly injure themselves.

I don't believe in any religion apart from *doing the will of God*. True, faith is the uniting link between Christ and the soul, but if we don't do the will of our Father, it will soon be broken.

See then that ye walk circumspectly, not as fools, but as wise .... understanding what the will of the Lord is.
EPHESIANS 5: 15,17

Set your heart on being a real saint and soldier of Jesus Christ. Go to Pentecost for your power, and to the apostles for your models. Don't take your type from those round about you; but as you refused to be satisfied with a one-sided gospel, so refuse to be conformed to a mermaid Christianity. If I mistake not, God has given you a mind and heart capable of high and holy resolve, self-sacrifice and enthusiasm; open it to the divine Spirit without fear of consequences. Say, *'Here am I. What wilt thou have me to do?'* And listen inwardly for the answer.

Time is flying; souls are perishing by thousands; men and women are dashing on the rocks which you have so recently escaped. Oh, warn, exhort, entreat! Get your heart fired with his love, and then, heeding not the trammels of conventionalism, or the dictates of worldly prudence, go to work for him and his lost ones.

May he help and guide you! Sheaves await your gathering which no one else can gather. Say not, *'I am a child.' 'I am with thee!'*

But the Lord said unto me, Say not, I am a child: for thou shalt go to all that I shall send thee, and whatsoever I command thee thou shalt speak.
JEREMIAH 1:7

CHRISTLIKENESS

All who know anything of the salvation of God must feel with me here, that if we cannot cover the earth with the knowledge of it, then we should cover as much of it as we can. That we are bound under obligation to do this seems to be self-evident to those who believe Christianity to be for the benefit of the race. Putting aside the future life altogether, I think we are bound to do this for the peace, purity, goodwill, beneficence, truth and justice which always follow in the wake of true Christianity.

Real Christianity is known by its fruits - peace, goodwill, purity, justice and truth. It inculcates and implants the love that worketh no ill of any kind to its neighbour, the love that seeks the good even of its enemies, and heaps the coals of fire of benevolence on the heads of those who hate it.

That is real Christianity, and wherever that goes, peace and goodwill are found. There can be no mistake about that.

For the kingdom of God is not meat and drink; but righteousness, and peace, and joy in the Holy Ghost.
ROMANS 14:17

TRUTH THAT CUTS

You must preach God's justice and vengeance against sin as well as his love for the sinner. You must preach Hell as well as Heaven. A gospel of love never matched anybody's soul. The great want in this day is *truth that cuts* - convicting truth - truth that convicts and convinces the sinner and pulls off the bandages from his eyes.

The Lord knew the order in which his truth ought to be preached better than we do. Hence his commission to Paul to go and *'open the eyes'* of sinners to their danger and turn them round from the power of Satan unto God. This was to be done before they were converted. *'Oh,'* says someone, *'don't talk to them about Hell, death and judgment; show them the love of Christ.'* But we always get it wrong when we reverse God's order. Tear the bandages off. Open their eyes; turn them round from the desire, the embrace, and the choice of evil to the embrace and choice of God that they may receive forgiveness of sins.

Tell them *the truth*; tell a man the truth about *himself*. Drive in the red-hot convicting truth of God on to his conscience and make him realise that he is a sinner. Never mind how he howls, even if he groans as loud as the psalmist did when the pains of Hell got hold of him. Until he has been made to feel himself a sinner, he will never make anything of a saint.

Then give him the gospel.

God hath made that same Jesus, whom ye have crucified, both Lord and Christ. Now when they heard this, they were pricked in their heart, and said unto Peter and to the rest of the apostles, Men and brethren, what shall we do?
ACTS 2:36,37

STANDARDS

God has reared a judgment seat in every man's conscience which in some slight measure answers to, and prefigures, the sentence which he declared he will pronounce on every man's action, whether it be good or bad.

Then if there be a great Judge at all, and a standard of right and wrong which he set up, it must be of supreme importance that we should correctly understand what is this standard and that we should judge the conduct of ourselves and of those around us according to it. Surely nothing could be more deceptive and soul-ruining than to accept as correct any short of the one unalterable and eternal standard of righteousness and truth which he has laid down.

What a sham to worship him who declares himself to be the way, the truth and the life, if there be no certain way, no definable difference between the true and the false, no practical separation between the Christ life and the life without Christ. Surely it is high time for all who care about the right of Christ on earth to make up their minds to one thing or the other.

If Christ be our Master, let us learn his lessons, and abide by his rule, and obey his commands.

The answer of a good conscience toward God.
1 PETER 3:21

CONSCIENCE

It seems to me that a great deal of failure in faith is simply the result of a defiled conscience, and if those who find themselves weak and sickly in spiritual life would turn their attention to the condition of their *consciences* they would soon discover the reason for all their failure.

Let us define conscience. Conscience is that faculty of the soul which pronounces on the character of our actions (Romans 2:15). This faculty is a constituent part of our nature and is common to man everywhere and at all times. All men have a conscience, whether enlightened or unenlightened, active or torpid, there it is: it cannot be destroyed. Therefore Christianity cannot propose to dispense with it, as God in no case proposes to *destroy* but to *sanctify* human nature.

There has been much philosophising as to the exact position of conscience in the soul - whether it be a separate faculty, as the will and the understanding, or whether it be a universal spiritual sense pervading and taking cognisance of all the faculties, as feeling in the body. It matters little which of these theories we accept, seeing that the vocation of conscience remains the same in both.

And herein do I exercise myself, to have always a conscience void of offence toward God, and toward men.
ACTS 24:16

AN INDEPENDENT WITNESS

Conscience is an independent witness standing as it were between God and man; it is *in* man, but *for* God, and it cannot be bribed or silenced. Somone has called it *'God's spirit in man's soul.'* All other of our faculties can be subdued by our will, but this cannot; it stands erect, taking sides against ourselves whenever we transgress its fiat.

Now it is a question of vital importance to our spiritual life whether the gospel is intended to deliver us from this reigning power of conscience, and make us independent of its verdict, or whether it is intended to purify and enlighten conscience, and to endow us with power to live in obedience to its voice. Let us examine a few passages on this point. First, let us see what is done with conscience in regeneration. *'How much more shall the blood of Christ, who, through the eternal Spirit, offered himself without spot to God, purge your conscience from dead works to serve the living God?'* (Hebrews 9:14. Second, let us see the office which conscience sustains in regenerate man. *'I say the truth in Christ; I lie not; my conscience also bearing me witness in the Holy Ghost.'* (Romans 9:1).

There are many other texts but these are abundantly sufficient to show that Paul had no idea of a wild, lawless faith, which ignored the tribunal of conscience. The apostles clearly show that true Christianity no more dispenses with conscience than it does with the great moral law by which conscience is set, and to which it is amenable.

I say the truth in Christ, I lie not, my conscience also bearing me witness in the Holy Ghost.
ROMANS 9:1

No Condemnation

The conscience must be made clean before it can be kept clean. The residuum of all sin settles on the conscience and, as all have sinned there can be no clean conscience by nature. There is only one way by which consciences can be purified. This can only be done by the blood of atonement. Every believer remembers the precious sense of purity and peace which spread over his soul when first he realised a saving interest in the blood of Christ; how sweet it was to feel that all the stains left by the sins of a past life were washed out - to realise that the anger and vengeance of an aggrieved conscience were appeased. The offence and condemnation of past sin is washed away, and now the conscience is void of offence, clean, and ready to serve the living God.

There is a beautiful significance in the word *'living'* in this connection; it seems to intimate that there is a fitness, an appropriateness, between the character of the Being to be served and the quality of that service. It is now not only made clean, but light, quick, tender, ready to detect and reject everything old, rotten, impure, unholy, and to keep it out of the sanctuary of the believer's soul as unfit for the service of the living God, who sees every thought, motive and desire.

And, oh, how true is conscience to its trust if only the soul would exercise itself *always* to obey!

Let us draw near with a true heart in full assurance of faith, having our hearts sprinkled from an evil conscience ...
HEBREWS 10:22

EFFORT

To maintain a conscience void of offence implies systematic obedience to the dictates of conscience. To be kept void of offence it must be obeyed with promptness; to parley is to defile. How many a soul has dated its ruin to temporising with a suggestion which conscience asserted ought to have been put down at once.

It requires unremitting effort, exertion, *'exercise'*, determination, *'Herein do I exercise myself'- the whole man - soul, mind and body - myself.*

Here is *'the fight of faith'*, *the* faith of the saints, which can dare and do and suffer anything rather than defile its garments. Only those who thus fight have the apostle's kind of faith. Satan knows this and he waylays such souls with every temptation possible to them. He tries considerations of ease, interest, honour, reputation, friends, fashion, health, life; and sometimes puts all these in one scale over against a pure conscience in the other.

It is no uncommon thing to meet with people in this condition who, *'having built again the things they once destroyed, have made themselves transgressors.'* Conscience is defiled and incensed, and demands that the evil shall be put away and repented of, and the soul cast afresh on the blood of atonement for pardon and healing.

Men and brethren, I have lived in all good conscience before God until this day.
Acts 23:1

CONSEQUENCES

Conscience is the reigning power of the soul, the will is the executive, and in order to keep a pure conscience the will must act on its teaching. When inclination lures, when the flesh incites to that which conscience condemns, the will must say No! and be firm. When Satan takes us up to the pinnacle and says, *'All these things will I give thee'* the will must say No! and repel the tempter.

This is just the point where human nature has failed from the beginning. Our first parents fell here. Their consciences were on the right side but their wills yielded to the persuasions of the enemy. This is sin. The committal of the will to unlawful self-gratification. Joseph's conscience thundered the right path and his will acted it out. Pilate's conscience also thundered the right course but his will failed to carry it out. In one we behold a hero, in the other a traitor.

This is the test of faith. Real faith dares trust God with consequences; a spurious faith must look after consequences itself! It must save its life whatever becomes of a good conscience.

This charge I commit unto thee, son Timothy, according to the prophecies which went before on thee, that thou by them mightest war a good warfare; holding faith, and a good conscience ...
1 TIMOTHY 1:18,19

COMFORT

I do indeed sympathise with you and I think I can divine a little as to the nature of your trials. I wish I were near to comfort and help you - such help as it is I have to offer. The only way of comfort I see for you is to try and walk *alone*, shutting your eyes to what you cannot help.

It is useless to harrow ourselves up about the past, or to waste time in vain regrets. It is past now, and can never be altered. but we can cast it under the blood, and go on praying him to avert the consequences, and maybe he will stoop to answer us. Do your own part in witnessing for God and truth, and hope that at some future time it will produce its effect.

Comfort yourself in the Lord. He is very pitiful and of tender mercy, and when he sees us truly penitent for our mistakes and failures he delights to pardon. Do not perplex yourself about the experiences of others. I am more than ever satisfied that God looks more propitiously on those who are striving and struggling to do right and to please him, even in fear and despondency, than on those who make light of sin and yet make their boast in him. I fear there are sadly too many who can rejoice when they ought to weep, while some who can never forgive themselves, weep when they ought to rejoice. Perhaps these latter are amongst those who, though they mourn now, *'shall be comforted'* hereafter.

And hereby we know that we are of the truth, and shall assure our hearts before him. For if our hearts condemn us, God is greater than our heart, and knoweth all things.
1 JOHN 3:19,20

AFFLICTION

There is no surer test for the Christian as to the state of his heart than the way in which he receives affliction. How often when all has appeared prosperous and peaceful, and the child of God has been congratulating himself on spiritual growth and increased power over inward corruption, has some fiery trial overtaken him. Instead of being met with perfect submission and cheerful acquiescence, it has produced sudden confusion, dismay, and perhaps rebellion, revealing to him that his heart was far from that state of divine conformity which he hoped and supposed.

Thus the Christian often suffers more from a consciousness of insubordination under affliction than from the affliction itself. Dear reader, how is it with you in this respect? When trials overtake you, are you able to say, *'It is the Lord, let him do what seemeth him good'*? Are you able to realise that *'whom the Lord loveth he chasteneth'*, and that these light afflictions are working a future increase of glory? If so, happy are you. This is the best of all evidence to yourself that the divine Spirit is working in you to will and to do of your Father's good pleasure.

If ye endure chastening, God dealeth with you as with sons; for what son is he whom the father chasteneth not?
HEBREWS 12:7

UNFAILING FOUNTAIN

If God dries up the water on the lake, it is to lead you to the unfailing fountain. If he blights the ground, it is to drive you to the tree of life. If he sends the cross, it is to brighten the crown. Nothing is so hard as our heart; and, as they lay copper in aquafortis before they begin to engrave it, so the Lord usually prepares us by the searching, softening, discipline of affliction for making a deep lasting impression upon our hearts.

> *The fire our graces shall refine,*
> *Till, moulded from above,*
> *We bear the character divine,*
> *The stamp of perfect love.*

The trials of your faith, being much more precious than of gold that perisheth, though it be tried with fire, might be found unto praise and honour and glory at the appearing of Jesus Christ.
1 PETER 1:7

THORN IN THE FLESH

The apostle says, *'I glory in my infirmities that in consequence of these the power of Christ shall so rest upon me as to lift me above them, so that I shall more glorify his strength and grace than if I were perfect in mind and body.'*

In another place Paul says, *'Lest I should be exalted above measure through the abundance of the revelations, there was given to me a thorn in the flesh, the messenger of Satan to buffet me.'* Some people think this was sin; but surely the words *'messenger of Satan'* show that this thorn was no act or disposition of Paul's but some external temptation or affliction inflicted by Satan.

Besides, the divine assurance, *'My grace is sufficient for thee,'* ought to forbid the idea of sin. Paul sought the Lord thrice to have this thorn removed; surely, if it had been sin, the Lord would have been as anxious to have it removed as his servant was. This thorn was, doubtless, some physical trial - as the words *'in the flesh'* indicate - some tribulation or sorrow through the patient endurance of which the strength of Christ could be magnified.

The Lord sent this to Paul not for the purpose of making him humble, for he was humbled before, but to keep him humble. And does he not send something to us all? Do we not need trials and tribulations in the flesh in order to keep us humble?

Lest I should be exalted above measure through the abundance of the revelations, there was given to me a thorn in the flesh, the messenger of Satan to buffet me ...
2 CORINTHIANS 12:7

TENDER MERCY

Affliction occupies a large place in the economy of salvation, for though suffering is the result of sin, God takes hold of it and transmutes it into one of the richest blessings of his own people. From whatever secondary causes the afflictions of the righteous may arise, whether from the sins of their forefathers, the cruelty of their enemies, their own mistakes, or the mistakes of their friends, or the malice of Satan, it is their blessed privilege to realise that the Lord permits and overrules all, and that he has a gracious end in every sorrow he allows to overtake him.

Happy the Christian who, though he cannot see this end at present, is able to trust in the goodness which chastens, and cleave to the hand that smites.

Behold, we count them happy which endure. Ye have heard of the patience of Job, and have seen the end of the Lord; that the Lord is very pitiful, and of tender mercy.
JAMES 5:11

Trial reveals us to God; makes manifest to him what is in our heart. Perhaps somone may object, and say, no, no, we need nothing to make manifest to God what we are, he understands us perfectly. He knows what is in man. True! and yet he says to Abraham, *'Now I know that thou fearest God, seeing thou hast not withheld thy son, thine only son, from me.'* And to the Israelites, *'And thou shalt remember all the way which the Lord thy God led thee these forty years in the wilderness, to humble thee and to prove thee, to know what was in thine heart, whether thou wouldst keep my commandments or no.'* Now God knew that Abraham feared him, and he also knew how far Israel would keep his commandments, but he did not know as a matter of *actual fact* until the fact *transpired*. He must have the latent principle developed in action before he could *know it as action*.

Thus Abraham by his obedience to the painful command made his love manifest to God. Not that God had previously any doubts of Abraham's love, but he desired a practical manifestation of it towards himself, or to know it in *action*.

The divine love is like all other love in this respect, it delights in practical proof of love in return, nor will it be satisfied without. Remember this, Christian , in thy various afflictions. Remember also that in nothing is love made so manifest as in willing cheerful suffering for the sake of its object.

Greater love hath no man than this, that a man lay down his life for his friends.
JOHN 15:13

151

THE MARTYRS

As the greatest manifestation of God to the world was by suffering, so the most influential revelations of his people to the world has been by suffering. They are seen to the best advantage in the furnace. The blood of the martyrs has ever been the seed of the Church. The patience, meekness, firmness and happiness of God's people in circumstances of suffering, persecution and death, have paved the way for the gospel in almost all lands and ages. A baptism of blood has prepared the hard and sterile soil of humanity for the good seed of the Kingdom, and made it doubly fruitful. The exhibition of the meek and loving spirit of Christianity under suffering has doubtless won thousands of hearts to its divine author, and tamed and awed many a savage persecutor, besides Saul of Tarsus.

When men see their fellow-men enduring with patience and meekness what they know would fill them with hatred, anger and revenge, they naturally conclude that there must be a different spirit in them. When they see Christians suffering the loss of things, and cheerfully resigning themselves to bonds, imprisonment and death, they cannot help feeling that they have sources of strength and springs of consolation all unknown to themselves.

And what shall I more say? For the time would fail me to tell of Gideon, and of Barak, and of Samson, and of Jephthae; of David also, and Samuel, and of the prophets: who through faith subdued kingdoms ... (of whom the world was not worthy:)
HEBREWS 11:32-33,38

TRIED BY FIRE

Do not be disheartened because you are tempted. Paul speaks of the fiery trials of the saints, of the fiery darts of the devil, and of being tried by fire. Now these must have been pretty sharp contests for such a brave soldier as Paul to call them fiery. Temptation is the severest of all tests of grace. Many a man could go to the block far easier than fight his own lusts.

Jesus knew this, therefore he warned his disciples against the first beginnings of sin (Matthew 5:28,29). Looking at, and thinking about, forbidden objects bring all our woe! Keep your eyes and your thoughts off, and you are safe. Jesus said, 'Watch'. Satan is cunning. He says, *'You can just indulge a little. You need not go all lengths.'* But he knows that if he can find a lodgment in the thoughts he is sure of everything. Mind him. He is a liar from the beginning. Resolutely resist his first whisper. Don't listen to one word. Run for your life. He has slain millions through the *first thought!*

Put on the whole armour of God, that ye may be able to stand against the wiles of the devil.
EPHESIANS 6:11

RIGHT WITH GOD

From the manner in which many speakers and writers arrogate all the civilisation in the world to Christianity, one would imagine that they had forgotten there was a civilisation in existence long before Christ appeared on the scene. I grant that civilisation follows in the wake of Christianity; but Christ did not come to *civilise* the world, but to *save* it and to bring it back to God. Ah! it was not his mission to cover up its moral sores by putting a respectable covering outside, while it remained full of rottenness and corruption. It was his misssion to cleanse away its vileness, to heal its moral wounds, and to restore soundness to its heart.

If I understand the Bible rightly, it appeals alike to civilised and uncivilised. It makes no distinction between the conditions of salvation nor the amount of salvation required by either. Jesus said to Nicodemus, who was one of the most highly civilised of his generation, *'Except a man be born again he cannot enter the kingdom of God.'*

Jesus Christ came, I say, to rectify men's hearts, and he persistently taught that this would rectify all his outward sorrows. That is, when you have got a man right with God, you will soon get him right with humanity, with himself, and in all his relationships with the world. I mean morally right. He will be physically wrong - outwardly wrong, for the world will persecute him; but he will be right in his relationships to it, for he will only live in it to mend it, and only have communications with other men in order to save them.

When Jesus heard it, he saith unto them. They that are whole have no need of the physician, but they that are sick. I came not to call the righteous, but sinners to repentance.
MARK 2:17

JESUS' EYES

I have been thinking how it is that Christians do not more fully realise their responsibility to extend the Kingdom of Christ and it occurred to me that one of the main reasons may be a want of realisation of the *danger* of the unsaved round about them. I am afraid that many get their brains so muddled by the different theories that are put forth about new hopes, eternal hopes, restorations, and I don't know what else, that they come to look upon a large class of their countrymen and the inhabitants of the world generally as, after all, not so far off the right way as the Bible represents.

They seem to forget that separation from God means death. They do not realise that these masses of people are, according to Jesus Christ's teaching, lost, and that unless some great renovation takes place in their souls, in their moral natures, they must perish; hence Christians grow indifferent and leave them alone.

I think the first thing necessary for those who are saved and right with God, is to look at the world as Jesus Christ looked at it, look at the multitudes and contemplate their condition, not letting their civilization, or education, or refinement divert us from the central fact that they are separated from God - dead in trespasses and sins - on the high road to Hell, and that nothing but the salvation of God can save them.

Behold, I say unto you, Lift up your eyes, and look on the fields; for they are white already to harvest.
JOHN 4:35

WE CAN DO IT!

Look around at the people everywhere! Think of them as away from God, as sunk in sin of one kind or another, and then say whether their necessity, their need ought not to prove your responsibility, ought not to be a call to you each one to put forth that effort to save them which is possible to you in whatever sphere or circle you may move.

We are individually responsible to save them because *we can do it.*

Some people are always trying to exalt God at the expense of man, throwing all the responsibility of their salvation of their fellow-men upon God and making nothing of human agency. I do not find God does so. I find that he makes a very great deal of man in the Bible; from beginning to end it is full of *'ifs'.* If you do this and that; if you fulfil my conditions; if you keep my commandments, such and such will follow. Right down from Adam to Paul, whom he commissioned to go and turn people from darkness to light, and from the power of Satan unto God, man is represented as an agent in his own and others' salvation.

Pray ye therefore the Lord of the harvest, that he will send forth labourers into his harvest.
MATTHEW 9:38

156

SAVE THE WORLD

A little thought will make us agreed, I am sure, that if greater progress in the effort to save the world is to be accomplished there must be a more efficient force to make it. God has arranged to save men by human instrumentality, and if we have not succeeded in the past, we are not to throw the blame on him, as too many Christians do. A man who was sitting in his easy chair with his feet on an ottoman, said to me only the other day, *'But the Lord will come presently and put all things right.'* I replied, *'I am afraid you are expecting the Lord to do what he has called us to do.'*

The Lord does not say he will go and preach the gospel to every creature; he says you are to do it. He does not say he is going to convert the world; he says you are going to do it. He has shown you the lines on which to work, and given you the resources, quite as much and more than he has given the agriculturist to cultivate and gather the fruits of the earth. If Christians were only half as diligent as husbandmen, the world would have been saved long ago.

Ye have not chosen me, but I have chosen you, and ordained you, that ye should go and bring forth fruit, and that your fruit should remain.
JOHN 15:16

SPIRITUAL FORCE

If we are to better the future we must disturb the present, which some people very much dislike. They would rather be let alone, though they know they are wrong. What is wanted, I say, is a force of spiritually equipped and determined men and women to take the world for God, men and women trained to the business.

Now, we want a force of men and women given up to this work, sworn to bring the world to Jehovah - bound together spiritually to God and to each other - that they will make it the business of their lives to subject the world to God.

Look at the world again. Here are the millions of men entrenched in their wickedness - entrenched behind all manner of refuges of lies, enamoured of their sins; some of gaiety, some of drink, some of impurity, some of ambition, some of money, some of learning, some of one thing and some of another. There they are, satisfied with their sins so far, because they won't allow themselves to think.

Oh, if men would only shake themselves up for an hour and face God and eternity they would not rest in their sins; but their great desire and the great object of the devil is to keep these things from them, so he keeps them always preoccupied, always busy.

I will say to my soul, Soul, thou hast much goods laid up for many years; take thine ease, eat, drink and be merry. But God said unto him, Thou fool, this night thy soul shall be required of thee ...
LUKE 12:19,20

EQUIPPED

We need men and women who are trained for the fight; not only people who have experienced a change of heart, but who are drilled in the use of the weapons of the Spirit - knowing how to handle God's truth. You would think if you heard some people's presentation of the truth of God that it was all honey and soap; you would not think there was any cut in it, any dividing asunder. A great deal of the truth preached nowadays would not cut the wings off a fly, much less pierce asunder soul and spirit.

Tell a man the truth about himself then the truth about God, then tell the truth about his obligations to others. That is, if you believe the things I have been saying are true. If you do not believe them, then do not go to chapel, do not have the Bible.

And those of us who have so far acted upon the truth as to give up the greater portion of our lives to the service of God, what will be our regret when we come to face eternity and look back on the past? That we have done so much? Oh, no; that we have done so little, that we have not made God and eternity the all-absorbing theme of our lives, that we have wasted any energy, time, or strength on less important things.

And take the helmet of salvation, and the sword of the Spirit, which is the word of God.
EPHESIANS 6:17

TONGUES OF FIRE

We are in the first of these passages expressly told that the women were assembled with the disciples on the day of Pentecost; and in the second, that the cloven tongues sat upon them *each*, and the Holy Ghost filled them *all*, and they spake as the Spirit gave them utterance. It is nothing to the point to argue that the gift of tongues was a miraculous gift, seeing that the Spirit was the primary bestowment. The tongues were only emblematical of the office which the Spirit was henceforth to sustain to his people. The Spirit was given alike to the female as to the male disciple, and this is cited by Peter as the peculiar speciality of the latter dispensation.

What a remarkable device of the devil that he has so long succeeded in hiding this characteristic of the latter day glory! *He* knows, whether the Church does or does not, how eminently detrimental to the interests of his kingdom have been the religious labours of woman; and while her seed has mortally bruised his head, he ceases not to bruise her heel; but the time of her deliverance *'draweth nigh.'*

These all continued with one accord in prayer and supplication, with the women, and Mary the mother of Jesus, and with his brethren.
ACTS 1:14
And there appeared unto them cloven tongues like as of fire, and it sat upon each of them.
ACTS 2:3

WOMEN AS WELL

God has promised in the last days to pour out his Spirit upon all flesh, and that the daughters, as well as the sons of mankind, should prophesy. And Peter says most emphatically, respecting the outpouring of the Spirit on the day of Pentecost, *'This is that which is spoken of by the prophet Joel!'* (Acts 2:16-18). Words more explicit, and an application of prophecy more direct than this, does not occur within the range of the New Testament.

Commentators say, *'If women have the gift of prophecy, they must not use the gift in public.'* But God says, by his prophet Joel, they shall use it, just in the same sense as the sons use it. When the dictation of men flatly opposes the express declaration of the *'sure word of prophecy'*, we make no apology for its utter and indignant rejection.

The Early Church fathers were slow to accept the fact that among the primitive Christians preaching was not confined to men, but that God had, according to his promise, on the day of Pentecost, poured out his Holy Spirit upon believers - men and women, young and old - that they should prophesy, and they did so.

The prophesying spoken of was not the foretelling of events, but the preaching to the world at large the glad tidings of salvation by Jesus Christ. For this purpose it pleased God to make use of women as well as men.

And it shall come to pass in the last days, saith God, I will pour out my Spirit upon all flesh: and your sons and your daughters shall prophesy.
ACTS 2:17

ALL ONE

As to the obligation devolving on woman to labour for her Master, I presume there will be no controversy. The particular sphere in which each individual shall do this must be dictatted by the teaching of the Holy Spirit and the gifts with which God has endowed her. If she has the necessary gifts and feels herself called by the Spirit to preach, there is not a single word in the whole book of God to restrain her, but many, many to urge and encourage her.

God says she *shall* do so, Paul prescribed the manner in which she shall do it, and Phoebe, Junia, Philip's four daughters, and many other women actually did preach and speak in the primitive churches. If this had not been the case, there would have been less freedom under the new than under the old dispensation, a great paucity of gifts and agencies under the Spirit than under the law, fewer labourers when more work to be done.

Instead of the destruction of the caste and division between the priesthood and the people, and the setting up of a spiritual kingdom in which all true believers were *'kings and priests unto God'*, the division would have been more stringent and the disabilities of the common people greater. Whereas we are told again and again in effect, that *'there is neither bond nor free, male nor female: for ye are all one in Christ Jesus.'*

There is neither Jew nor Greek, there is neither bond nor free, there is neither male nor female: for ye are all one in Christ Jesus.
GALATIANS 3:28

FRY AND FLETCHER

Notwithstanding all the opposition to female ministry on the part of those deemed authorities in the Church, there have been some in all ages in whom the Holy Ghost has wrought so mightily that at the sacrifice of reputation and all things most dear, they have been compelled to come out as witnesses for Jesus and ambassadors of his gospel. As a rule, these women have been amongst the most devoted and self-denying of the Lord's people, giving indisputable evidence by the purity and beauty of their lives, that they were led by the Spirit of God.

Now, if the word of God forbids female ministry, we would ask how it happens that so many of the most devoted handmaidens of the Lord have felt themselves constrained by the Holy Ghost to exercise it. The word and the Spirit cannot contradict each other. Either the word does not condemn women preaching or these confesseedly holy women have been deceived.

Will anyone venture to assert that such women as Mrs. Elizabeth Fry or Mrs. Fletcher of Madeley have been deceived with respect to their call to deliver the gospel message to their fellow-creatures? If not, then God does call and qualify women to preach, and his word, rightly understood, cannot forbid what his Spirit enjoins.

I commend unto you ... our sister, which is a servant of the church ... that ye receive her in the Lord, as becometh saints, and that ye assist her in whatsoever business she hath need of you: for she hath been a succourer of many.
ROMANS 16:1,2

HERITAGE

What sort of training does God, and our duty to our children, require of us? In order to get at the answer to this question, the first important matter for a parent to settle is this: To whom does this child belong? *Is it mine, or is it the Lord's?* Surely this question should not need any discussion, at least by Christian parents. For do we not recognise, even before they are born, that they are peculiarly and exclusively a heritage from the Lord, and when they came into the world, the first effort we put forth was to hold them up and offer them to him?

And again, in our baptismal vows, we acknowledged that they belonged to him, and promised to train them for his glory. Now the keeping of this one fact before the mind will be the best guiding principle in training; and it is because Christian parents so often forget whose their children are that they make mistakes in training them.

I say then, settle it in your minds that your child belongs absolutely to God, not to you - that you are only stewards for God, holding your children to nurse them and train them for him.

This responsibility arises, firstly, out of the command and ordination of God. Both under the old and new dispensations, the Lord has laid the obligation on parents to train their children for him; he commands it, to whom both parents and children belong.

For this child I prayed; and the Lord hath given me my petition which I asked of him: Therefore also I have lent him to the Lord; as long as he liveth he shall be lent to the Lord.
1 SAMUEL 1:27,28

MORAL EXCELLENCE

Obedience to properly constituted authority is the foundation of all moral excellence, not only in childhood, but all the way through life. And the secret of a great deal of the lawlessness of these times, both towards God and man, is that when children, these people were never taught to submit tot the authority of their parents; and now you may convince them ever so clearly that it is their duty, and would be their happiness, to submit to God, but their unrestrained, unsubdued wills have never been accustomed to submit to anybody, and it is like beginning to break in a wild horse in old age.

There is seldom need for chastisement where mothers begin early and wisely. There is a way of speaking to and handling an infant compatible with the utmost love and tenderness, which teaches it that mother is not to be trifled with; that, though she loves and caresses, she is to be obeyed, and will be obeyed, and a child that is trained in this way will not, as a rule, attempt to resist. In exceptional cases it may be tempted to become obstreperous, and then the mother must show her authority.

For whom the Lord loveth he correcteth; even as a father the son in whom he delighteth.
PROVERBS 3:12

USE YOUR AUTHORITY

Do not be afraid to use your authority. God has sent your child to you to be guided and restrained by your *authority*, as much as to be inspired and encouraged by your love. How do you answer for the neglect and abuse of this wonderful power? You will recollect the fearful punishment that came upon Eli, one of the most terrible strokes of vengeance recorded in the whole Bible. What was it for? Not for using profane language before his children, for he was a good and righteous man, but *'because he restrained them not'*; that means he did not use his authority on the side of God and righteousness.

Parents, if you fulfil your part of the covenant, never fear that God will perform his. Only you train your children truly for him, and *he* will charge himself with their future; but do not expect, if you neglect your sacred trust, or abuse it by training them in the nurture and admonition of the world that God will work a miracle to convert them when they come to mature years because you cry and pray and ask him to do so. He makes no such promise.

For I was my father's son, tender and only beloved in the sight of my mother. He taught me also, and said unto me, Let thine heart retain my words: keep my commandments and live.
PROVERBS 4:3,4

TRUST AND INTEGRITY

Another important point in training a child in the way he should go is to train him in the practice of truth and integrity. Human nature is said to go *'astray from birth, speaking lies'*, and doubtless, untruthfulness is one of the most easily besetting and prevalent sins of our race. To counteract this tendency, and to establish the soul in habits of truth and sincerity, must be one of the first objects of right training. In order to do this, parents should beware of palliating or excusing the tendency of falsehood in their children.

No mother will succeed in begetting in her child a greater antipathy towards any sin than she *feels for it herself.*

Children are quickest of all analysts and instinctively detect in a moment all affectation of goodness. They judge not so much from what we say as *how we feel.* They are not influenced so much by our teaching as by our spirit and example. Take the trouble to make your children *true*, and God will enable you to do it. If you *work for him* with your children, he will work *with you* in them, and you shall have the joy of seeing them grow up into Christ.

... The acknowledging of the truth which is after godliness.
TITUS 1:1

EXERCISES IN DEVOTION

To train a child in the way it should go we must not stop with those qualities and virtues which bear on man, but it must be trained in the exercises of devotion and piety towards God. Of course, none but truly Christian parents are equal to impart *this* kind of training. The Holy Ghost must needs be in the heart of the mother who undertakes to lead her child to God. The bias to evil is too strong to be turned aside by unassisted human wisdom or strength, however great. But there is every encouragement to those parents who are truly his to hope for success in training their children for him.

When I call to remembrance the unfeigned faith that is in thee, which dwelt first in thy grandmother Lois, and thy mother Eunice; and I am persuaded that in thee also.
2 TIMOTHY 1:5

There is a sense in which the children of believers are already set apart for him. Many parents seem to lose sight of this covenant relation, and bring up their children under the idea that they must needs live in sin till they come to 15 or 16 years old, and then they hope God will convert them in the same marvellous and sudden manner in which drunkards and profligates are converted.

Now I am a firm believer in conversation as any one can be, and I also believe that the children of believers need to be converted as much as others, but I say this is not the way to teach our children to expect it. What is conversion but the renewal of the mind by the Holy Ghost through faith in a crucified Saviour? And if there are *'diversities of operations by the same Spirit'*, why may not the minds of children be renewed very early? If the will of a child be sincerely yielded to God, cannot the blessed Spirit as easily and as effectually renew and actuate its heart and affections as those of an adult?

And does not Jesus say, *'Suffer the little ones to come unto me'*?

But Jesus said, Suffer little children, and forbid them not, to come unto me: for of such is the kingdom of heaven.
MATTHEW 19:14

CHILDREN

Of what advantage would it be to train a child in the *'nurture and admonition of the Lord'* if he did not purpose to bless this training to their conversion and salvation? The very terms of this injunction show the sense in which the Holy Spirit uses them. *'Nurture'* means *'nursing, feeding, strengthening, developing'*. *'Admonition'* means *'reproof, caution, instruction.'* Here is the order of God, firstly, the feeding and strengthening of all that is good in them; and secondly, the reproof and caution against evil; and thirdly, instruction in righteousness.

If parents would only take the Lord's way, they would see their sons and daughters taking their places in the temple of the Lord, as their natural and abiding home.

And, ye fathers, provoke not your children to wrath: but bring them up in the nurture and admonition of the Lord.
EPHESIANS 6:4

A FATHER'S LOVE

I conceive that the first idea, the very foundation of a religious training, should be to impress the young heart with a sense of God's *fatherhood*, his tenderness and love toward mankind generally. The young soul should be *drawn towards God*, not repulsed from him. Work this conviction into the mind of a child and *then* show it the obligation it is under to regard God's will in all things and to keep his commandments (not failing to explain their import and spirit, according to the child's understanding) and the conscience of even a little child will testify to their reasonableness and righteousness. Let these two ideas, first God's fatherhood and love, second the obligation arising out of this relationship to keep his commands, take possession of the mind of a child and they will produce a sense of moral degeneracy far *deeper* and more influencial than could be produced by any other means.

If the parent or teacher were continually reiterating the fact of his being a sinner from morning to night, in the child's ear, it would produce no consciousness of it in his heart, but let him be *thus* instructed and he will *feel* bitterly that there is antagonism between his soul and God's holy law. He will understand better the nature and consequences of sin than all the abstact teaching in the world could explain, and thus will the foundation of true conversion be laid deep in his own experience; for when the plan of redemption comes to be unfolded to his mind and heart, he will at once receive it as in harmony with his settled ideas of God's character. He will look upon it as an expression of a Father's love rather than a scheme to appease an angry judge.

If ye then, being evil, know how to give good gifts unto your children, how much more shall your Father which is in heaven give good things to them that ask him?
MATTHEW7 :11

171

FELLOWSHIP

There are precious enjoyments, holy, heavenly, felicitous enjoyments, which we have never dreamed of or conveived. One is a knowledge and love of God, a blessed association and fellowship with him. What does it mean? It means association and happy intercourse with God's people on the common ground of love for, and likeness to, the Saviour, telling of God's grace, the trials you have gone through, the victories you have achieved, and getting down on your knees and, as my husband calls it, *'going to Heaven together.'*

> *I have been there and still would go,*
> *'Tis like a little heaven below.*

There is no stiffness, no stately introduction; in five minutes we are spiritually hugging one another, blending our tears and songs and prayers as the heart of one. If you find out such a meeting, go to it; it is a pity they should be so few and far between.

Another of these joys is doing the will of God, of labouring for Christ. There is more joy in taking up the cross for Jesus, in suffering for him, than you ever had in your whole lifetime. The joy of praising him is inexpressible - it is too rich and hallowed and holy, too much like the joys of Heaven, to be portrayed in human language - you must know it and realise it.

And let the peace of God rule in your hearts, to the which also ye are called in one body; and be ye thankful.
COLOSSIANS 3:15

172

EVERLASTING BLISS

What can be a fitter cause for enthusiasm than the religion of Jesus Christ? Why, the mere fact that our sins have been forgiven is enough, surely, to stir us to the very uttermost extent we are capable of. When the apostles were rejoicing over the subjection of the devils to them, they seemed to have a great reason for gladness, but Christ says to them, *'Rejoice rather because your names are written in Heaven.'*

And then we are privileged to enjoy communion one with another. I am afraid that the idea of the communion of saints is little understood nowadays. There is but little, I fear, of that close, personal, religious conversation, that enquiring into the well-being of one another's souls which used to be so highly valued. But wherever such communication takes place, *'as iron sharpeneth iron, so doth the countenance of a man his friend'*, and, consequently, the communion of saints must always tend to promote enthusiasm.

But even individual enjoyment of God and divine things must, where carried to any great extent, result in an enthusiasic state of feeling. The soul occupied with God must get into a condition something like that expressed by the hymn, which says:

> *My willing soul would stay*
> *In such a frame as this,*
> *And sit and sing herself away*
> *To everlasting bliss.*

And let us consider one another to provoke unto love and to good works: Not forsaking the assembling of ourselves together ... but exhorting one another ...
HEBREWS 10:24,25

FERVOUR

The world hates hot saints because they look with contempt on its pleasures, set at naught its maxims and customs, trample on its ambitions and applause, ignore its rewards, abjure its spirit, and live altogether above its level. It can tolerate warm religionists - rational, decent people who appreciate this world as well as the next, and can see how to make the best of it - but these *'hot, pestilent, mad fools'* who obtrude their religion everywhere, who are at everybody about their souls, who are always talking about God, death, judgment, Heaven and Hell - *'away with them, they are not fit to live.'*

To be hot ensures opposition from the devil. Oh, how he hates these hot saints! What trouble he takes to trip them. He knows they are worth it. Many a council is held in Hell over these. They set fire to his standing corn. They rout his best legions. They shake the foundations of his throne. They take the prey out of his very jaws; they pull it out of his fires.

He *must* do something! He sets his principalities and powers to work on them. Loose and feeble fiends will do for lukewarm people, but these he must take in hand himself and try all the guile and force of his gigantic intellect on them. But let me remind you, that to be hot ensures God's special favour, protection and fellowship, and our final victory.

Not slothful in business; fervent in spirit; serving the Lord.
ROMANS 12:11

174

HEAT CLEANSES

Heat cleanses, purges away dross, destroys noxious vapours. So the burning fire of the Holy Ghost purifies the soul which is filled, permeated with it, hence hot saints are pure. They purify themselves, as he is pure. Their garments are white, they keep themselves *'unspotted from the world'*. They improve the moral atmosphere wherever they go. Their very presence reproves and holds in check the unfruitful work of darkness, and sinners feel as Peter felt when he said, *'Depart from me, for I am a sinful man, O Lord.'*

But who may abide the day of his coming? and who shall stand when he appeareth? for he is like a refiner's fire, and like fuller's soap.
MALACHI 3:2

HEAT BURNS

Heat burns. Hot saints set on fire the hearts of other saints. They singe the consciences of sinners, burn the fingers of the Pharisees, melt the hearts of backsliders, and warm up those who have left their first love.

Who maketh his angels spirits; his ministers a flaming fire.
PSALM 104:4

HOT SAINTS

Hot saints are mighty. The Spirit is not given by measure unto them. They may not be very intellectual or learned, but their heat makes more impression on the hearts of sinners, and stirs more opposition from Hell than all the intellect and learning of a whole generation of lukewarm professors.

The fishermen of Galilee produced more impression on the world in three years than all the learning of the Jewish had done in centuries, because they were *hot* in the love and service of God.

Hot saints are more than a match for their enemies.

And there appeared unto them cloven tongues like as of fire, and it sat upon each of them. And they were all filled with the Holy Ghost ... And they were all amazed and marvelled, saying one to another, Behold, are not all these which speak Galileans?
ACTS 2:3,4,7

THE FIRE

But by what power is victory achieved? BY FIRE! The Holy Ghost. Fire is the most potent force in nature. Electricity, light, heat - all are fire. Everything must give way before fire. *'Some trust in chariots and some in horses'*, but our trust is in the living fire - the Holy Ghost - to burn up our enemies inside and melt down or frighten away our enemies outside.

All we want is enough of this fire and whole towns shall shake at our approach and all Hell affrighted at our advance. True, we have a mighty task before us, but we have a mighty force.

The time has come for fire. All other agents have been tried: intellect, learning, fine buildings, wealth, respectability, numbers. The great men and the mighty men and the learned men have all tried to cast out these devils before you and have failed. TRY THE FIRE! There are legions of the enemies of our great King. Fire on them.

There are the legions of strong drink, damning millions; of uncleanness, millions more; of debauchery, blasphemy, theft, millions more! Charge on them, pour the red hot shot of the artillery of Heaven on them, and they will fall by thousands!

Hear me, O Lord, hear me, that this people may know that thou art the Lord God, and that thou hast turned their heart back again. Then the fire of the Lord fell and consumed the burnt sacrifice ...
1 KINGS 18:37,38

PEACE

What kind of kingdom would you expect where Christ reigned? In the first place, the principles laid down by him, the Lover and Saviour of men, would be acted upon everywhere. There would be truth. Every man would speak the truth with his neighbour. There would be righteousness. Men would deal justly with one another. Man's enmity to man brings our greatest sorrows. When men love God first and their neighbour as themselves, there will be an end to extortion, and oppression, and cruelty, and injustice. There will be universal happiness and joy. It needs no particular fresh adjustment of things to make men universally happy. Remove sin and you will very largely remove suffering from the earth.

There will be universal peace. There will be peace in every house, peace and goodwill to every man, peace in every city, peace in all our borders. When the Prince of peace shall rule over the kingdoms of this world, they will learn war no more. They will be done tearing each other's hearts out. They will live in peace and unity.

Our Father which art in heaven, Hallowed be thy name. Thy kingdom come. Thy will be done in earth, as it is in heaven.
MATTHEW 6:9,10

CHRIST ENTHRONED

What kind of a kingdom would you expect where Christ reigned? There will be universal recognition of and rejoicing and boasting in the Lord. No more shame-faced religion! No more hypocrisy. Everybody will be real. Everybody will be glad to express allegiance to him. His subjects will not be ashamed to procession in the streets. Every man and woman among them will be shouting his praises and openly glorifying the Lord that reigneth.

You say, *'Yes, it is a beautiful picture, but, like many others, it is impossible.'* Do not say, *'impossible'* for God says it shall be. May he help every one of his saints to do all they can in bringing the King back to his own world and getting everybody to love and serve him.

There will be an end of the *'bitter cry'* business. Here is the solution of the great social problems about which some of you are vexing your souls. PUT GOD ON THE THRONE! And then everything will come right.

At the name of Jesus every knee should bow, of things in heaven, and things in earth, and things under the earth; and that every tongue should confess that Jesus Christ is Lord, to the glory of God the Father.
PHILIPPIANS 2:10,11

HARD WORK

God has always blessed the right kind of devotion. In the darkest ages, when his true saints were trammelled by the falsest opinions and ideas, he always showed himself to be a willing co-worker with anybody who would help him to save anybody else. Therefore, we have only to get on the right lines, and avail ourselves of the divine power and give that divine power fair play, and we will turn the world upside down.

But there is only one way and people don't like it. We are a lazy race. Tens of thousands of people lose half the best things of life for want of trouble. They do not like hard work. It is just so in divine things.

The Church has been trying for ages past, with conferences, holding of synods, its councils and church meetings, groaning, praying, and sentimentalizing, to get this done in an easy way. It is not done yet, and it never will be done in that way. There is but one way of getting victory, and that is by desperate, hard, determined, persevering fighting.

Blessed be the Lord my strength, which teacheth my hands to war and my fingers to fight.
Psalm 144:1

COMPASSION

We must fight with ignorance by enlightening it. We must come down to that measure of humiliation and sacrifice which is necessary to this. We must adapt ourselves. We must grapple with the condition of the people where *they are*, put the arms of a loving sympathy around them, and weep tears of Christlike compassion over them, man to man, woman to woman, in hand-to-hand, face-to-face conflict.

We must contend with hatred and opposition BY LOVE, show sinners how God loves by our love, by our willingness to sacrifice and suffer for them; make them see it in our tears, in our prayers, in our trudging about after them, in *'Christ's stead beseeching them to be reconciled to God.'*

Do you ever take such a measure with any poor, dark soul as could be rightly interpreted *'beseeching'*?

Now then we are ambassadors for Christ as though God did beseech you by us: we pray you in Christ's stead, be ye reconciled to God.
2 CORINTHIANS 5:20

MAKE HASTE!

We must fight fully consecrated. No more soldiers saying, *'I will fight if you will guarantee I shan't be shot!'* No more soldiers saying, *'Well, but where will you send me? Will the air agree with me? What sort of fare shall I get?'*

Fully consecrated. *'Here I am, Lord Jesus, to be your man or your woman for any service you want of me; to go down into the world, to stand at the mouth of the cannon, to go down into the trenches, in the coldest climate, or to trudge across the desert sands.'*

There used to be such soldiers. You have read of them. You wept over the pages and laid the book down and said, *'I wish I were such an one.'* BE ONE! BE ONE! You say, *'Oh, if we could get up a mighty force of such soldiers!'*

Make haste! Get it up.

Thou therefore endure hardness, as a good soldier of Jesus Christ
2 TIMOTHY 2:3

CONFLICT

Who ever heard of aggression on the territory of an enemy without opposition. Such a thing is impossible naturally, and still more impossible spiritually. *'The whole world lieth in the arms of the wicked one.' 'The strong man armed keepeth his goods,'* and if we are armed by a stronger than he, we must expect opposition.

Our Lord systematically taught his disciples to expect and prepare for persecution. He taught them that their principles, motives, and objects, would be so incomprehensible to men of a worldly spirit, whether Pharisees or worldings, that they would inevitably persecute and oppose them.

I take it as one of the worst signs of the Christianity of this age that it provokes so little opposition; for it is as true now as it ever was, that if we are not of this world, the world will hate us; and that he that is born after the flesh will persecute him that is born after the Spirit.

Blessed are ye, when men shall revile you, and persecute you, and shall say all manner of evil against you falsely, for my sake.
MATTHEW 5:11

REVIVAL

The Church *might have* a revival as wide and deep and powerful as she asks, if she would only comply with the conditions on which God can grant it - if she would remember her unfaithfulness, honestly confess and forsake her sins, and bring into God's storehouse the tithes of which she is so flagrantly robbing him. But it is easier to utter vain repetitions and leave the responsibility of the damnation of souls upon God, than for Christians to humble themselves, confess before the world their fallen and powerless condition, and pay their vows unto the Lord.

The Lord only wants a whole-hearted faithful people and the walls of Jericho would fall and a nation be born in a day. Oh, may the Lord send upon his backsliding Israel the spirit of convicting and of mourning! May he open her eyes to see from whence she has fallen, and enable her to repent until her iniquity is purged, her backslidings healed, and her lips touched with living fire from off his pure and holy altar.

Wilt thou not revive us again: that thy people may rejoice in thee?
PSALM 85:6

WARFARE

Christ's soldiers must be imbued with *the spirit* of the war. Love to the King and concern for his interests must be the master passion of the soul. All outward effort, even that which springs from a sense of duty, will fail without this. The hardship and suffering involved in real spiritual warfare are too great for any motive but that of love. It is said that one of the soldiers of Napoleon, when being operated upon for the extraction of a bullet, exclaimed, *'Cut a little deeper and you will find my general's name'*, meaning that it was engraved on his heart. So must the image and glory of Christ be engraven on the heart of every successful soldier of Christ. It must be the all-subduing passion of his life to bring the reign of Jesus Christ over the hearts and souls of men.

A little child who has this spirit will subjugate others to his King, while the most talented and learned and active, without it, will accomplish comparatively little. If the hearts of the Christians of this generation were inspired with this spirit, and set on winning the world for God, we should soon see nations shaken to their centre, and millions of souls translated into the Kingdom.

But thou, O man of God, ... follow after righteousness, godliness, faith, love, patience, meekness. Fight the good fight of faith ...
1 TIMOTHY 6:11,12

COMMITMENT

The soldiers of Christ must be *abandoned to the war*. They must be thoroughly committed to God's side: there can be no neutrals in this warfare. When the soldier enlists and takes the Queen's shilling, he ceases to be his own property, but becomes the property of his country, must go where he is sent, stand at any post to which he is assigned, even if it be at the cannon's mouth. He gives up the ways and comforts of civilians and goes forth with his life in his hand, in obedience to the will of his sovereign.

If I understand it, that is just what Jesus Christ demands of every one of his soldiers, and nothing less.

No man that warreth entangleth himself with the affairs of this life; that he may please him who hath chosen him to be a soldier.
2 TIMOTHY 2:4

VICTORY

The soldiers of Christ must *believe in victory*. Faith in victory is an indispensable condition to successful warfare of any kind. It is universally recognised by generals of killing armies, that if the enthusiasm of expected conquest be destroyed, and their troops imbued with fear and doubt as to the ultimate result, defeat is all but certain. This is equally true with respect to spiritual warfare, hence the repeated and comprehensive assurance and promises of victory from the great Captain of our salvation.

The true soldier of Christ has an earnest in his soul of coming victory. He knows it is only a question of time, *and time is nothing to love!* The faithful soldier *knows* that he shall win and that his King will ultimately reign, not only over a few, but over all the kingdoms of the earth, and that he shall reign till he has put all enemies under his feet.

This faith inspires him to endure hardship and to suffer loss, to hold on. He listens and above the din of earthly conflict he hears the words, *'Be thou faithful unto death, and I will give thee a crown of life.'*

But thanks be to God, which giveth us the victory
through our Lord Jesus Christ.
1 CORINTHIANS 15:57

THE VOICE OF GOD

God wants the answer. The voice which some of you have heard for months and years as distinctly as it ever rang in the soul of any prophet: *the voice of God in your soul.*

To begin with, you *know* it is the voice of God. It matters not what human instrument it has come through. If God had used a sparrow or some inanimate instrument to convey his message, that would not take away for a moment the importance of the message, or render it optional as to whether you would return an answer. *What is the answer to be?* Perhaps some of you say, *'I do not choose to return an answer.'* But it is not optional with you whether you will or not.

All truth coming from God demands an answer from every soul who listens to it; that very refusal to return an answer is an answer of defiance. It is saying back to God, *'Mind your own business. I don't want your will. I have chosen my path. I am busy about other matters. I shall not return any answer to your messages.'* That very attitude is an answer of defiance. You cannot help yourself; your soul *must* respond to the truth one way or the other.

You have heard that inward voice; you have seen that inward light. Now you must say *'Yes'* or *'No'*. You can never go back to where you stood before - never!

Also I heard the voice of the Lord, saying, Whom shall I send, and who will go for us? Then said I, Here am I; send me.
ISAIAH 6:8

189